JOURNEY INTO DOLPHIN DREAMTIME

Horace Dobbs

JONATHAN CAPE
LONDON

To my mother

First published 1992
© Horace Dobbs 1992
First paperback edition published in 1993 by
Jonathan Cape, 20 Vauxhall Bridge Road, London SW1V 2SA

Horace Dobbs has asserted his right
under the Copyright, Designs and Patents Act, 1988
to be identified as the author of this work

A CIP catalogue record for this book
is available from the British Library

ISBN 0–224–03092–2 (hardcover)
0–224–03739–0 (paperback)

Phototypeset by Computape (Pickering) Ltd, North Yorkshire
Printed in Great Britain by
Mackays of Chatham PLC, Chatham, Kent

Contents

Illustrations

No one can bear too much
reality. To look at life without
illusion is like looking at the
sun without a filter

Anthony Daniels

· I ·

Sunrise at Uluru

The vapours hovering above the summit of the smoothly rounded peak were the first to feel the transforming force of the beacon of life that was creeping slowly up behind the horizon and tinting the sky above it with amber light. Three blackfellas, still as statues, stood silently watching, waiting for the moment when the sun spirit would touch the sacred stone itself and once again perform the miracle of turning night into day. Then the highest tip of the rock, that reached up to the very eye of the heavens, caught the sun and sucked it downwards. Slowly a golden glow flowed down the rock face leaving the cool night spirits to recede into dark crevices where they hid from the light of the dawning day. Like a blossom coming into bloom, Uluru, or Ayers Rock as it was known to the whitefellas, responded to the sun spirit that awakened the day. Not until they could feel its warm hands gently stroking their backs did those blackfellas standing on the flat plane move away. No words were exchanged. They were unnecessary. The blackfellas walked ahead in line. The leader did not have to look down to know where to place his feet. After years of walking the bush he automatically used his peripheral vision subconsciously to perceive any obstacles on the track or the presence of any animals nearby while he looked straight ahead, searching out the route to their destination.

The spirits of the three blackfellas mingled with those of the rocks, the trees and the gullies, all of which were brought into relief by the invading sun. The Aboriginal men were adrift in the Dreamtime. Their Dreamtime journey was not bounded by space or time. It started before they were born and would continue after they were dead.

Having embraced Uluru, the sun spirit swept on across the Australian continent in a tidal wave of sunlight. On its daily journey it engulfed stringy bark trees, transforming the tough boughs of eucalyptus leaves from purple to olive green. It raced past animals, heavier than humans, that were bounding across the landscape as if on giant springs. Secure inside the pouches of the females, newborn babies, like passengers in a mobile milk bar, sucked at tiny teats. Blind and smaller than fieldmice, the naked neonates were cocooned at a constant temperature against the ravages of the blistering sun and the dangers of dingoes. In contrast, newly hatched emus had to forage for themselves from the moment they broke out of their shells. Although feathered, they would never take to the air, and would have to rely on their sharp eyes, strong beaks and long legs to avoid trouble. They inhabited the scrub where, powdered with ochre dust, they blended with the ground. Their rounded bodies were difficult to distinguish from the bushes into which they could disappear and through which they could scurry with deceptive speed.

In its headlong rush over the barren landscape the advancing sun crossed flat beds of grey minerals deposited by evaporating ponds. It tinted with gold isolated black-trunked trees whose ancient boughs, tough as teak, bent into arches that touched the ground. One hour and twenty minutes after leaving Uluru the advancing edge of brilliant light reached the end of its trans-Australian passage and streaked out into the Indian Ocean.

At Shark Bay, about 700 km (400 miles) to the north of Perth in Western Australia, it gilded the dorsal fins of a group of dolphins cruising in shallow water over a plain of dark seagrass close inshore. The dolphins were moving slowly towards a whitefella from England who was standing in the sea at the edge of a land that two hundred years earlier had been inhabited only by blackfellas.

He had woken at first light and made his way to the beach

to commune in silent reverence, like the blackfellas, with the awakening day. He stood alone at the boundary between the land and the sea. To the east behind him the land mass of Australia extended for 4,000 km (over 2,000 miles). Ahead lay the Indian Ocean, an apparently endless mass of sparkling water that stretched for more than 7,000 km (some 4,500 miles) round the Tropic of Capricorn to the coast of Madagascar off the continent of Africa. He stood where the land animals handed over the sun spirit to the sea creatures.

As the tide surged gently in and out it moved the sand beneath his feet, gently sucking them down until he was rooted into the seabed like a tree. Not until the sun had risen over the edge of the earth did he move. The dolphins detected the sound of his stirring and swam towards the beach to make their first human contact of the day.

There was a time, earlier in their Dreamtime, when only blackfellas came to the beach. Because they were closely related the spirits of man and dolphin blended easily. On departing into their respective worlds of land and sea, each carried the image of the other with them. When the blackfellas wandered back into the bush, they gathered around camp fires to pass on their knowledge, using words and music to mix and mingle their experiences like the ingredients in a cake until they all became one with Dreamtime. Thus the dolphins became woven into a tapestry of the spiritual and physical life of the indigenous population of Australia. The beach where the meetings took place was added to the sacred sites that speckled their landscape. Unlike the monuments created and dedicated to gods by other civilisations, these were invisible to the naked eye. Details of their location and significance were guarded and passed on by very special elders who, without the benefit of maps and written words, retained the precious information in their prodigious memories.

The dolphins generated high-pitched sounds to form a vision of what was around them, recreating sound pictures when passing stories of their meetings with the Aborigines to other dolphins they met far offshore. But that was long ago, and for many years no humans came to this special meeting place. The dolphins, also possessing vast memories, thought that humans had abandoned the sacred site. But after a time fresh contact was made with other tribes of humans – white, not black. At first it was not of a spiritual nature, like that with the blackfellas, but then many who came began opening up again the channels that led into Dreamtime.

Drawing lines across the bay, like sunbeams converging towards the sun, other dolphins slipped towards the point of interspecies communion where the whitefella was pulling his feet out of the sand. When they arrived he kept his arms by his side and allowed the dolphins to extend their own invitation for physical contact. Using their pectoral fins like fingers, they brushed his submerged legs with a feather-light touch. Only after they had welcomed him into their domain did he respond. Bending over and cupping some water in his hands, he allowed it to dribble on to the back of the dolphin at his feet which had raised its head above the water and nodded a greeting, its open mouth briefly revealing a pink tongue and almost a hundred conical teeth. Three more dolphins milled around, silently tracing random patterns in the water with their dorsal fins. When another person paddled into the sea further along the beach, they moved off, leaving the man to continue his one-to-one communion with their fellow.

As more and more people sauntered down to the sea the dolphins, cruising back and forth, greeted them. The babble of excited human voices grew until it overwhelmed the murmur of the gently heaving sea. The light hardened. The long soft shadows became shorter and sharp-edged. When the man finally made his way from the beach, it was bustling with a melee of children and grandparents, splashing in the sparkling water, all excited at the prospect of seeing and touching the dolphins. The man appeared to be unaware of the transformation that had taken place. His soul was adrift, like a spent rocket in the timeless tranquillity of outer space.

I was that whitefella.

Although the concept of Dreamtime was new to me, two centuries ago it was not new to the Australian Aborigines, or for that matter to the American Indians, who lived fulfilled lives in which the spirit of all things, whether animal, vegetable or mineral, was as important and identifiable as their physical characteristics. The way in which these people used their brains – anatomically almost identical to mine – was fundamentally different from that of modern western man. They could be as intelligent but their intellects functioned in another mode. Mine was a strictly logical mind; at least, I thought it was. From my first meeting with Donald, a friendly wild dolphin, I had tried to be objective and assess and interpret what I had seen of dolphin/human interactions by means of the tenets instilled in me during my studies at London University and in a scientific career that spanned chemistry, physics, biology, human medicine and veterinary medicine. Yet none of these disciplines could explain what I was observing, nor – perhaps more important – what I was feeling inside.

A map drawn by an Aborigine portraying a mind vision of his home territory in the Australian outback bore no resemblance to the ordinance survey style of representation which was meaningful to me. In my world everything had to be clearly explained and neatly separated into well-defined compartments that could be juxta-posed rationally to produce a mental picture, like a mosaic. But in theirs thought processes derived from a widely diverse range of inputs merged to give a continuous holistic mental image of both space and time.

In my culture everything that could be measured was measured. An object or an idea had real significance only if it could be quantified in units, like money, which everyone could understand. We had become as obsessed with gathering facts as we were with acquiring wealth. In the Dreamtime qualities such as aesthetic appeal, which were subject to individual variation that could not be measured, were the dominant criteria for making judgements. Even time, the ultimate measurable phenomenon which I could identify in hundredths of a second, was comprehended in a different way. In the Dreamtime the past, the present and even the future came together inseparably.

For me, entering the Dreamtime was like finding a new space in my mind that hitherto had lain hidden behind a door to which the dolphins provided the key.

The spinning earth ensures that the sun is always on the move around our planet. Twelve and a half hours after torching the sacred rock candle, Uluru, in the heart of the Australian desert, the Sun Woman who – according to Aboriginal legend – carries the sun across the sky, allowed her flame to light the tip of the mast of a catamaran anchored a short distance off a long sandy beach.

The sea was calm and the vessel barely rocked in the almost imperceptible swell. Below, in one of the twin hulls, the skipper lay sleeping. As a mother becomes aware of the needs of her baby during the night so the subconscious mind of the experienced sailor is always alert, ready to detect a noise or movement that could signify danger. An approaching squall will change the movement of the waves and cause the mariner to wake immediately.

As the dawn light descended the mast the skipper became aware that something was bumping against the hull. It was the small tender, tied to the stern, which he had used the previous evening to row back to his floating sleeping-quarters. Yet the sound was not the random gentle thud that went unnoticed when he was asleep; this was a deliberate bump, bump, bump, like someone knocking on a door. And that is precisely what it was. Except that in this case the someone was a friendly dolphin paying an early morning social call.

In an instant, the sailor was awake, ready to spring out of bed and take whatever action might be necessary to avert the peril to which his sixth sense had alerted him. As his eyes came into focus and accommodated to the sight of the familiar surroundings of his small cabin so his ears analysed the sound that had woken him.

'Oh, it's you, JoJo,' he said out loud. 'What time do you call this? Don't you know I had a late night last night?'

For a moment he felt like rolling over and going back to sleep; but he didn't. He had made a pact with the dolphin. No matter what time of day or night the dolphin called he would leave what he was doing and go for a swim with him.

Sometimes the dolphin would call in the middle of a dark moonless night and the two of them would streak through the water creating whorls of phosphorescence that were so bright they could see one another in the inky darkness. At other times the dolphin would come streaking across the water when the skipper was sitting on deck with a group of friends. At such times the dolphin might announce his arrival with a couple of leaps. It was an open invitation for an aquatic game. They were all invited into the sea to play.

The sailor and the dolphin had many things in common. Both were aquatic, and both nomadic; they were independent loners. As a result of the time they spent together a bond had been forged between them that was stronger and more deeply emotional than that between many a human couple bonded by wedlock.

The man was supremely fit, had a fine slim physique and was as brown as a walnut from hours spent sailing in the Caribbean. He was a land-based mammal raised in a city who had used his large brain to assimilate knowledge about the wind, the waves, and the tide. He had applied it to the design of a Polynesian-style catamaran which he had built with his own hands in a faraway land. When the task was completed, the boat became a physical extension of his body, enabling him to sail away from the confines of his urban environment. He knew the anatomy of his boat better than that of his own body. Every plank, cleat, rope, every inch of sail was familiar to him. It was a living thing, and with it he harnessed the energy of the wind, like a seagull.

It was the twin hulls cutting parallel furrows across the sea that had first attracted the dolphin. Now the dolphin was as familiar with the two floating islands and the man who controlled them as he was with the contours and inhabitants of the reefs he regularly patrolled. When the dolphin raced forward under the netting between the hulls, he could sense and feel the closeness of the human above him.

The man gazed down at the speeding form beneath him and marvelled at the effortless way the dolphin slid through the water, apparently defying the laws of hydrodynamics which he had been taught when studying boat design. The knowledge he had so painstakingly acquired served to amplify the joy and respect he felt for the creature which sought his company. The presence of the dolphin and the curving lines it traced through the pale blue space of the sea set his spirit soaring. What value had possessions compared with freedom and beauty such as this? As he watched and marvelled at the sheer perfection of shape and movement he understood why, in ancient times, dolphins were revered as gods. He also realised he was privileged, and this was why he felt he had to respond when the dolphin summoned him to play by thumping his tender against the hull of his boat.

A few moments after hearing the signal he dived over-board into the coral sea. The crests of the ripples on the surface caught the newly arrived rays of sunlight and sent them zig-zagging into the depths, transforming the gloomy reef into a sparkling underwater wonderland. The sun was the signal for the fishes that had retreated into the deep recesses in the coral during the night to exchange places with the nocturnal feeders who browsed the reef during the hours of darkness.

Holding his breath, the man pulled himself through this awakening world with powerful strokes of his muscular arms, enjoying the refreshing sensation of water streaming across his naked body. Through his open eyes he saw the blurred images of purple fans that waved slightly as he passed. He was careful to avoid brushing against the deep-red latticed stinging coral or colliding with the sharp tips of the Stag Horn coral as he flew through the undersea garden with the looping, swooping flight of a sparrow. Around him sped the dolphin with the swiftness and unerring accuracy of a feeding swallow, interspersing long curving sweeps with sudden sharp changes of course. Sometimes the dolphin swam at full speed towards the man. Then, when a catastrophic head-on collision seemed inevitable, the dolphin would change course, missing his playmate by a pencil's width. It was a well-practised tournament in which they both engaged their swimming skills and stamina to the limit. The man knew full well that an intended blow from the dolphin's beak could be fatal, but he had long since passed the stage where he had any fear that the dolphin would either deliberately or accidentally strike him. Their spontaneous, passionate undersea ballet was a ritual in which they expressed their love and their trust in one another. It lasted until the man could no longer sustain the pace.

When the exhausted but jubilant sailor climbed back on to his floating home the dolphin recognised that the game was over and did not tarry. JoJo had plenty of energy left and immediately moved away, cruising purposefully along the reef while listening intently. He was hoping to detect the special sound made by another of his human friends who was out for an early morning swim and was signalling the dolphin to join him. As JoJo swam towards his next human encounter he could feel the sun, white and intense, warming his back through the transparent water.

The dolphin and the rising sun would affect many human lives. Memories of the sun's touch would fade with the skin tan, but an encounter with a friendly, frisky dolphin was something all those who met JoJo that day would remember for the rest of their lives.

When the sun arrived at the island of Providenciales (or Provo, as it was usually called) dusk was falling in central Australia. By the time the dolphin had finished his dawn frolic and was traversing the sea in dazzling light the three blackfellas at Uluru had become part of the night-time Dreamtime. That was when a black carpet was rolled across the sky and the moon sprinkled seeds of light on to it.

During the day a stranger had arrived at their camp. He

was from a faraway tribe. One of his totems was unusual – a dolphin. Furthermore he was an elder – a venerated man with much wisdom.

Music, dance and storytelling rituals are at the core of Aborigine tribal culture. Corroborees take place at night. So when Mother Sun had extinguished her flaming torch at the end of the day, a fire was lit and all of the tribe at the camp gathered round. The orange tongues from the blazing sticks crackled as they licked the black sky. The sound of chanting, pricked with the sharp staccato crack of clapsticks, rose steadily like an incoming tide. Flooding waves of sound washed away all conscious feelings. The bodies of the blackfellas ceased to exist. Their spirits linked with those of their ancestors, and they all became one with the Dreamtime. Then, flowing through the night like the dark brown muddy waters of the mighty Mississippi River, rushing forward with uncontrollable power and then eddying into flat smooth swirls, came the sound of the didgeridoo. Through its mystical voice the stranger carried his audience on a journey along a Songline. It was a long spiritual voyage through many sacred gullies and past sacred rocks, ending in a water space so big you couldn't see the land beyond. At this place, the ocean, there were extraordinary fish and animals unlike anything seen before.

Bringing the images of dolphins into his mind, and blocking out all other thoughts, the itinerant visitor continued to blow into the sacred hollow tube. Through the sounds of his didgeridoo he created spirits of dolphins and floated them into the minds of the blackfellas gathered round the fire.

They continued to chant when the wailing of the didgeridoo ceased and the stranger disappeared behind a bush, where he had placed a bag containing his few possessions. Here, unseen by human eyes, he painted some wavy lines on his already decorated body. When he re-emerged he was no longer a human; he was fish-shaped. He was a dolphin rising out of the waves and breathing with an audible sharp suck through a nose on the top of his head. By means of this mime and dance the blackfellas came to know how the dolphins were incorporated into the Dreamtime.

Enthralled with the new dimension he had added to their lore, the tribe joined together in a dance, raising clouds of dust with their stamping feet. They became one with the features of Uluru, the giant rock of Ayers that towered behind them, its daytime colours hidden beneath the coal-black paint of the night. To the gathered Aborigines, Uluru was a living cathedral. Hundreds of Dreamtime events were permanently retained within and without its huge body. Each mark, each crack, each stain had an explanation in the Dreamtime.

Before the corroboree started the elders of the tribe realised that the visitor was a 'karadji' – a man with a huge fund of sacred knowledge of which he was one of the special custodians. With his knowledge and power he could travel back through the millennia to the time when the Great Spirit Ancestors of the Dreamtime first sang the world into existence. With their dance and song the blackfellas added another precious fragment to the 40,000-year-old culture the stranger carried with him on his Songline journey through the island continent of Australia.

· 2 ·

Woolly Bear

The sea holds many mysteries. One of the most puzzling of them is why some dolphins abandon the company of their fellows and seek contact with humans instead. From the human viewpoint it seems a naive and utterly foolish thing to do. Our record is one of indiscriminate slaughter of species of all kinds, from the buffalo to the bustard. The large whales, in the same order (*cetacea*) as the dolphins, have been brought near to extinction by man. So why should a reputedly intelligent animal like a dolphin make a deliberate move to offer us humans close friendship? Could the fact that dolphins have brains as large and complex as ours make them capable, in theory at least, of behaving mentally and emotionally like us? Is it the challenge of the unknown that motivates them? Do these friendly solitary wild beings have something like the 'Everest urge' to drive them – not from necessity – into exploring new frontiers despite the dangers and the risk of premature death?

Speculation will doubtless continue until we can communicate fully with dolphins. Meanwhile we can only go by the ever-increasing documentary evidence that identifies from our side what circumstances lead to first contacts and how the relationships subsequently develop.

A dolphin worthy of special attention in this respect is one that by 1991 had provided Ireland with its largest single tourist attraction, pulling in hard currency in millions both directly and indirectly. Seven years earlier John O'Connor and his daughter Dierdre first sighted the dolphin on 14 April while snorkelling off the coast near Dingle. The creature was curious but cautious, quietly watching them as it drifted into and out of the hazy limit of their underwater vision. It was the largest mammal they were ever likely to encounter at close quarters in the sea. The two snorkellers were excited and just a little apprehensive.

Afterwards John telephoned the news to his diving buddy Ronnie Fitzgibbon who lived in Tralee, the capital town of County Kerry and famous the world over for its annual Rose of Tralee Festival. Ronnie closed his diving shop and headed for Dingle where the following evening he and John set out to see if the dolphin was still in the area. They found it – or, to be accurate, the dolphin found them – off Beenbawn Strand where dolphin and divers watched each other apprehensively from a safe distance. There was tension and excitement on both sides but the first threads of friendship were formed. Just as a rope is strengthened with each thread that is added, so the bond between the adolescent dolphin and the two mature divers grew each time they met thereafter.

When John and Ronnie made inquiries, they discovered that the dolphin was already known to local fishermen, for he sometimes escorted their boats when they approached and left Dingle harbour. The fishermen called the dolphin Funghie, but nobody could remember exactly why he had been given such an unusual name. One explanation has it that the dolphin was first spotted off a headland upon which mushrooms grew. It seemed far-fetched but, whatever the explanation, Funghie was the name they eventually adopted.

At first the dolphin did little more than escort the divers' boats, riding the bow waves for a time as they swept out beyond the lighthouse. If the dive site was not too distant the dolphin would join the divers briefly underwater, zooming out of the mist and whizzing past them. Occasionally he would hesitate for a few moments, watching them intently before rushing away. And as the seasons passed so the trust and the interest the dolphin had in his undersea visitors built up.

One of the favourite excursions for the sub-aqua enthusiasts when they were fully trained was a drift dive on the incoming tide through the straits below the lighthouse. They would roll off the inflatable just outside the harbour entrance, sink to the bottom, and then let the current carry them effortlessly along. It was an exciting way to travel, especially if the dolphin visited them as they flew across the seabed. The boat would follow their bubbles, and when the divers surfaced they would make their way into a bay opposite the lighthouse where everyone could enjoy a surface swim with the dolphin. This gave even more divers a chance to meet Funghie because the bay was completely sheltered from the predominantly south-west winds which could make the sea rough and uncomfortable at Beenbawn. Even so, the presence of the friendly dolphin was virtually unknown outside the community in Dingle and the divers of the Tralee Sub-Aqua Club.

In May 1986 John O'Connor wrote to me briefly reporting the dolphin's presence, and as a result I published a request for more information and pictures.

Sheila Stokes and Brian Holmes, who lived in Cork and were both divers with a passion for dolphins, sent me a description of the solitary dolphin which had played with them for four days in the water near Dingle. They included with their letter some photographs which showed just how close their encounters had been. They had seen no one else swimming with the dolphin and believed they were the first to establish close contact.

Unsure of the creature's sex, Sheila and Brian had named it Dorad, the Gaelic word for dolphin. They kept detailed notes of the weather, the sea conditions, and of course the dolphin's behaviour, in an attempt to study as scientifically as they could the development of a relationship between a wild dolphin and two humans. With my previous experience with solitary friendly dolphins I was in a good position to help them in this task, and on 29 October 1986 I crossed the Irish Sea in severe Gale Force 9 winds to see for myself how their endeavours were progressing.

It was what the Irish term 'a soft day' – misty, with everything dripping wet – when we arrived in Dingle, parked our cars beside a ruined folly and made our way on foot across muddy fields to the automated land-based lighthouse, where we were greeted by the retired keeper Paddy Ferriter, his menagerie of cats, and a bouncing dog called Boka. From this high viewpoint we could see that the dolphin was in the water just below us. Before long Sheila had on her wetsuit and was descending the rocks to say hello to her friend Dorad. Brian followed and I joined them a short time later.

The sky was dark and a fine drizzle added to the gloom. It was close to high water and the sea had the unwelcoming colour of a cross between battleship grey and dark blue. Visibility was about ten feet (three metres) and the dolphin came up to inspect me. I remained motionless in the water with my arms extended and looking down. I was aware that I was being examined closely by the dolphin which swam quietly round me at a distance of about three feet (one metre) before moving in closer. Eventually he came round to the front of me and hovered, vertical in the water, with his beak only an arm's length from my face-mask, his eyes peering into mine. I just floated and felt a great joy well up inside me; I hoped the dolphin would accept me as a friend. It was a very beautiful, gentle experience.

Twice, when the dolphin was close to me, it turned belly-up. In these fleeting moments I tried to identify the sex. My views of the abdomen were brief, but even so I felt fairly certain Dorad was male, and not female as Sheila and Brian had tentatively suggested.

During the three-quarters of an hour I spent in the water Dorad's obvious apprehensiveness at having a stranger present gradually diminished. He stopped the intimate play with Sheila in which he had engaged when she was alone with him in the water and divided his attention between the three of us.

When we returned next day, Dorad appeared slightly nervous, but he soon regained confidence. I was wearing black neoprene gloves and extended one hand sideways. He examined it very carefully, and when I waggled my fingers, he responded by nodding his head vigorously. Then he took off at great speed and surprised my diving partners by rearing over them and whizzing past. He returned and pushed hard against my hand with his beak before departing again at great speed. This was an important event because it was the dolphin who had taken the initiative to make the first direct physical contact with me.

Dorad was quite scarred, and I noticed a number of short white marks near the blowhole which looked as if they had been caused by him rubbing the top of his head against the rocks. He liked to be scratched and would swim past in such a way that I could stroke his entire body with my gloved hand. If I tried to hold the dorsal fin he would get even more excited, but he would not allow me to grip it. Even so, I did not feel that this was upsetting him.

Whenever and wherever a hermit dolphin appears it invariably attracts publicity. This leads to the impression that such occurrences are common, but of course they are not. They are very rare and present unique opportunities for extended studies which otherwise would not be possible of the behaviour of an animal in its natural habitat. One person who appreciated this was Biddy Baxter, the producer of the BBC's longest running children's television programme, 'Blue Peter'. Despite my warning that the dolphin could disappear at any time, she decided to risk the absence of one of her chief presenters for two days, and the expense of a full film crew, in the expectation that we would return with material that would maintain, and even enhance, the long tradition of 'Blue Peter' as an informative, entertaining and adventurous programme. As a result I arrived at about nine o'clock on Tuesday 15 September 1987 at Milltown House in Dingle, just as Caron Keating was finishing her breakfast. Despite the fact that she had done a live television show the previous evening in London, had flown to Shannon and then been driven to Dingle, she looked as bright as a daisy. Her accent immediately identified her origins as Irish, but from north of the border.

After breakfast the filming and diving equipment was loaded on board *Tuna*, a boat I had used on several earlier visits to see the dolphin. It was skippered by Laurence Benison, with help from his wife Jeannie and son Mike, who handled the Zodiac inflatable which was to serve as our safety boat. We crossed the harbour and entered the channel that led into Dingle Bay, scanning the water for the dolphin as we went. Not until we were in the open sea did we get our first fleeting glimpse of a triangular fin. The dolphin had made contact. We anchored opposite a cave in the steep cliffs with rocks hanging like a folded curtain around its entrance, and Caron and I prepared to go in.

The dolphin, who was familiar with the routine when the *Tuna* anchored, knew what would happen next – or thought he did. The anchoring procedure was usually quickly followed by the entrance into the water of someone to play with him. Despite all the activity on this occasion, however, there was nothing interesting from the dolphin's point of view. This was because we were busy filming Caron kitting up. By the time we were ready the dolphin had become bored and disappeared. Mike was despatched in the inflatable to see if he could find the dolphin and entice him back. Caron had already grown chilly in the very thin wetsuit designed for windsurfing by the time Mike returned with the dolphin following close behind. When she slipped into the water, the cold took her breath away. Her new facemask kept misting up and she felt nervous as well as uncomfortable when she began talking to camera on the boat. She was unaware that the dolphin had swum up to greet her from behind. Receiving no response from the figure in the water, he disappeared again to set about the serious business of catching his lunch.

The shivering presenter stayed in the water until she could take the cold no longer and climbed back on the *Tuna*. Warm in our professional wetsuits, John (the underwater cameraman) and I swam over to the rocks where a thrashing tail on the surface indicated the dolphin's hunting ground. As we approached he rose with a silvery salmon weighing about 5lbs in his mouth. Three times he threw the fish high in the air, playing with it and obviously showing off. Then the dolphin swam away.

When eventually he reappeared, the dolphin swept past me with an impish grin but no fish. I assumed he had eaten it. Once again he vanished into the haze, then seconds later was back with the same fish clamped between his teeth. Deliberately he showed it to us, departed and returned almost immediately without the fish. Perhaps I had been mistaken and it was a second fish he had just consumed. When he returned again with the fish in his mouth after another brief interval, I guessed that he was hiding it somewhere and going back to retrieve it. The next time he zoomed out of the haze I watched where he went and hastened after him in the hope that I might locate the salmon before he did. I never found it. But the dolphin found me, materialising out of the mist once more, this time to swallow the fish, head first, right in front of me. It took several gulps before the tail finally disappeared down his gullet and left the sea sparkling with silvery scales.

The second day's filming went perfectly. Caron now knew what to expect and was much happier and more relaxed in the water. The dolphin seemed to sense her confidence. After examining her from behind, where she couldn't see him, Dorad (as we called him in the programme) swam round to peer into her facemask and I was able to film the two of them together with my underwater camera. The meeting did not last long but I knew that I had enough to convey to a young audience the excitement and joy Caron experienced in those short moments with a wild dolphin. By one o'clock we had got what we wanted and were heading back to the jetty.

That afternoon Caron had to fly back to London to present a live edition of 'Blue Peter' the next day. All the members of the film crew were reluctant to leave, especially those who had not been able to get into the water with the dolphin. Some said they would return to Dingle in the summer, but I was more fortunate for Laurence had invited me to join him for a relaxed expedition the following morning.

Like a Polar bear emerging from winter hibernation in a hollow beneath the snow, I slowly travelled from the dark, empty, space-filled void of unconscious sleep into an awakening day. Embraced in the cocoon of the duvet, my first sensation was its touch, gentle as a warm wind upon my face. Then, out of the cream-coloured light that dazzled my vision, the room took shape and the red poppies on the curtains came slowly into focus. By a magical act of recreation, I was aware and alive; born again into another day – a luminous blank page with verses yet to be written.

From the bedroom window I looked out at a tranquil vista. In the far distance I could see the white stub of the lighthouse. There was no fringe of swirling white surf at the base of the dark cliffs upon which it stood, nor on the other side of the harbour entrance, so I knew it was calm out at sea. In the foreground a million dewdrops on the lawn and on the bowed heads of the dahlias sparkled in the early morning sunlight.

While I wallowed lazily into life, others were already astir. Laurence and Jeannie Benison, who lived close to the water's edge, were already preparing for a day at sea aboard the *Tuna*. It was ten o'clock by the time I arrived at their house and found them ready and waiting to go to sea. Laurence quickly ferried me in the inflatable to the *Tuna*, motionless at her moorings, where I was greeted by Jeannie and her crew. A few moments later the engine throbbed into life, the mooring rope was slipped and we were heading as smoothly as a toboggan across ice towards the harbour entrance. As I was free from the need to do any filming for the BBC, Laurence said the day was to be entirely mine in which to do whatever I liked. It was during this conversation that Jeannie said rather wistfully how she had longed to go into the sea with the dolphin.

'Why on earth don't you?' I said. 'There's a spare wetsuit in the cabin.'

Taking Jeannie into the water to swim with the dolphin would give the day a sense of purpose and banish the twinge of guilt I felt, as usually I did whenever I set out simply to enjoy myself.

'I don't want to interfere with your day,' Jeannie said. 'I can go out at any time when you've gone.'

'Nonsense,' I retorted, touched as always by her unselfish consideration. 'It's a perfect day. Today's the day.'

As if to add his weight to the argument, the dolphin surfaced alongside and exhaled loudly.

'You see! The dolphin wants you to go in.'

Laurence had an endearing habit of giving everyone on the *Tuna* a nickname, and one of those crewing for him that day often wore a one-piece thermal jumpsuit known in the diving community as a woolly bear – so Woolly Bear she was called whenever she was aboard. We anchored opposite the cave entrance and I decided to shoot some cine-film of Jeannie's introduction to the dolphin. With Woolly Bear in the water to give her confidence, Jeannie stepped from the *Tuna* into the inflatable and then slid gently in beside her.

I started to film from the *Tuna*, but soon stopped. I had neglected to take into account the dolphin's habit of examining new visitors from below and usually from behind. While Jeannie floated on the surface, apprehensively waiting for the dolphin to appear, she was unaware that he was beneath her, examining her legs and navel. I could see what was happening but knew that the shadowy image of the dolphin beneath the surface would have no impact on film. After a few frustrating moments, during which the dolphin did not even surface to take breath, I abandoned surface filming and joined Jeannie in the water.

She was a little nervous and you could tell that the dolphin was aware of this. Eventually she let go of the side of the inflatable and we swam together towards the cave entrance, where the dolphin paid us a few fleeting visits. Jeannie was gaining confidence by the minute and I was delighted for her sake that she had made the decision to meet the dolphin in the sea. When she started to feel chilly I urged her not to stay in the water any longer. A warm diver is a happy diver, but if a diver is chilled the sea takes on a different, more hostile character. When Jeannie left the water, I put on my aqualung and sank beneath the surface to take pictures of Woolly Bear playing with the dolphin over my head.

The dolphin did not give us his entire attention for he was preoccupied with fishing for an early lunch. He visited us between snacks and these moments of high exultation when he played with us were heightened by the quiet intervals when he disappeared to feed. An hour passed before we climbed back aboard the *Tuna*, with the sea ruffled by a rising wind and clouds obscuring the previously clear blue sky. Jeannie, exhilarated and moved by her first encounter with a wild dolphin, made steaming mugs of tea to banish the chill from our limbs.

As I was not due to return to England until late the following day we decided to take the *Tuna* out again next morning, weather permitting, for one last swim with the dolphin. Scarcely had we loaded everything aboard before Jeannie went below to get into a wetsuit. She was raring to get into the water, as was Woolly Bear, who emerged from the cabin shortly after Jeannie wearing a semi-drysuit which would keep her warm for much longer than Jeannie's thin windsurfer's wetsuit.

At first I thought we would do some filming by the natural rock archway well outside the harbour entrance but, when we anchored, the swell rocked the boat in such a way that I knew it would be very uncomfortable for those left on board. We raised anchor and headed back towards my favourite cave opposite the lighthouse.

I got into the water first and was quickly followed by Jeannie. To ensure that her mask would not mist up, I had rubbed the inside with sea soap and then washed it out. The day before she had also found it difficult to grip the snorkel in her mouth, so I found her a new one and spent some time making sure she could breathe easily without water flooding in when she dipped her head just below the surface.

'Dolph is coming to see you,' Laurence said to his wife as

she hung on to the side while I adjusted her mask.

As soon as they were completed she swam away from the boat towards the gully that led to the cave. The dolphin knew at once that she was much more confident than on the previous day. I was wearing full diving equipment and had inflated my buoyancy compensator while attending to Jeannie. When I saw how easily she was finning away from me, I pulled the toggle that released the air from the inflated jacket and sank gently down, feet first.

I enjoyed the feeling of weightlessness and breathed easily from my aqualung. I could see Jeannie above me, attached to the silver ceiling like a hydrogen-filled balloon. Beneath her the dolphin circled curiously. I filmed the two of them with my cine-camera and then switched to stills. Everything was working perfectly, and the magic of the morning continued to build. The dolphin became more exuberant when Woolly Bear jumped into the sea. He leapt over the snorkellers and then swam round them vigorously. For almost an hour they enjoyed each other's company before Jeannie began to feel cold and reluctantly climbed back into the boat.

Having handed to Laurence the aqualung and all of my photographic equipment, I made it clear to the dolphin that I wanted to play. Dolph responded immediately, hurtling round the gully that led into the cave. From my position in the middle I could see his entire circuits. Bobbing up and down, I felt like a ringmaster, though I was not cracking a whip and was being circled not by trained horses but by an untamed wild dolphin. He circled with the speed and exuberance of a wall-of-death motor-cycle rider. Faster and faster he went swirling through the kelp, leaping over Woolly Bear who was floating spellbound close to the rocks.

I duck-dived and finned as hard as I could to the surface, managing to get most of the trunk of my body out of the water. Then I stopped finning and allowed myself to sink down. This delighted the dolphin who came up beneath me, pushing against my fins with his beak and partially opened mouth. He started to thrust harder, propelling me faster and faster through the water.

I was encapsulated in a bubble of excitement. Nothing else in the world existed except the dolphin and me. The sun beamed down into the water and beneath us the green kelp swayed. We were building to a crescendo. Having pushed me with his beak, the dolphin leapt over me. I whirled round in the water, finning as fast as I could and rotating my body like a top. I was a grandfather, yet here I was playing like a young child.

Repeatedly I stroked the dolphin as he swept past, and then I put my arms around him. He remained vertical in the water and allowed me to cling to him as he quivered. A wild dolphin was allowing me to embrace him. Such was the emotional intensity of the moment that I felt it could not have been greater had we been two lovers coming together in the open sea. Woolly Bear, who watched the whole scene, said that the dolphin went into a spasm of ecstasy.

Once again, by discarding my habitual preoccupation with achievement and just playing, I had advanced my relationship with a dolphin in the open sea to an extent that I would have said only a few years earlier was impossible for any human being. It was an overwhelming culmination to the 'Blue Peter' week. But that was not all. When I discovered later that Jeannie was 72 years old, I couldn't help wondering with such a spirit of adventure alive in her what escapades she had got up to earlier in life.

The Dingle dolphin was fast becoming a superstar. Most of those who visited him told their friends. Those who made the journey to see the dolphin were not disappointed. Sue Jones hitch-hiked from Dublin. 'It took all my good sense to stop myself running to the edge of the cliff and leaping into the water,' she wrote describing her reaction on first sighting the dolphin. Sue Rush confided her experiences and emotions in her diary and sent extracts to friends.

Tuesday: Today I climbed inside a dream and it became reality. The dolphin does exist – he is more beautiful than any other living creature on this planet. With his playful actions and a cheeky smile, who could help but fall in love?

Gently he unfolded his personality to me, teasing me and tempting me to get bolder. I look down and see he has passed beneath me and his great fluke is under my face. I say in my head, 'This is not wise', but I have an over-whelming sense of security, curiosity and happiness. This master of the sea will not falter, his fluke will not even brush my face, I am quite safe but I have a feeling of respect and I sense his power.

Suddenly, like a torpedo, he is heading straight for my mask. From full power to perfect stillness I didn't see a muscle move. He has stopped one inch away from the end of my nose. He is smiling. His eyes are bright. He knows he has played a trick on me. Eye contact is intense and quite intimate. I am lying still. I look at him and he looks at me, staring straight at me. 'Who are you? What are you? What is your game?' I know there is a set of needle-sharp teeth inches away from my face, yet I am transfixed and motionless, and so is he. Suddenly I feel great excitement welling up inside me as he rolls under me, belly up, and I see an upside down smile . . .

An hour passed like blinking.

Others who fell under the dolphin's spell expressed their feelings in verse and song. The guitarist Larry Conklin was inspired to produce an album called 'Dolphin Grace'. Action images of the dolphin's joyful leaps illustrated numerous stories that appeared in the press. One feature in the *San Francisco Chronicle* reported the dolphin of Dingle harbour as attracting television crews, divers and scientists from around the world ' . . . the dolphin provides hours of enter-tainment, boosts the local economy, serves as a symbol of good fortune and is even thought to restore health to chroni-cally depressed people.' Film units arrived from as far afield as Japan.

'Dolphins just seem to bliss out humans – they certainly

I-2 Bottlenose dolphins live in different environments, ranging from coral reefs in the Caribbean to kelp forests in the Atlantic

3-4 I did not know that Jeannie Benison was over 70 when she braved the cold water to have her first swim with the friendly dolphin in Dingle Bay

elicit the best from me,' was how New Zealander Tom White described what stimulated him to visit Dingle.

It was in Dingle, of course, that I launched Operation Sunflower and shot the television film *The Dolphin's Touch* which showed how the dolphin helped to lift three people out of clinical depression. The story of the making of that film is told in my book *Dance to a Dolphin's Song*.

Bill Bowell was a changed man as a result of his dolphin encounters. He had not worked for twelve years and was being treated for chronic depression at the Radcliffe Infirmary in Oxford. Dr Kim Jobst, an Oxford University Squibb Research Fellow at the Department of Clinical Neurology, was so impressed by Bill's recovery that he decided to investigate 'the dolphin effect' for himself. He took his senior research nurse Elizabeth King, zoology student Paula Hill, and a fellow doctor who was very sceptical, to Dingle to experience at first hand an encounter with a dolphin. Dorad, alias Funghie, had a positive effect on the entire party. He enchanted them, but just how the dolphin had helped Bill out of depression remained a mystery to them.

Bill was not at all concerned about *how* dolphins worked their magic. He considered himself living proof of the value of dolphin therapy and was grateful that he had been helped out of what he called his 'black pit'.

For me, the film opened up still more searching questions. In his book *Love, Medicine and Miracles* Dr Bernie Siegel suggests that all disease can be traced back ultimately to a lack of love, or to a depression of the immune system due to experiencing only conditional love. So is the 'unconditional love' that many have reported experiencing when swimming with Funghie the secret of the dolphin's healing powers? How important is the release of pent-up emotions? Is overcoming fear of the sea or of the dolphin a key factor? Does the dolphin set up the beneficial energy fields that some researchers in the United States see as crucial to the proper functioning of the nervous system and of the brain? Are dolphins in some way telepathic? Do the ultra-sonic sounds they produce stimulate the release of endorphins? How these endorphins, our natural bio-chemicals, regulate pain relief, joy and well-being is described by Deva and James Beck in *The Pleasure Connection*. Are there even more possibilities? I obviously had to keep my options open.

My search for the essence of dolphin therapy was made no easier by the fact that almost everyone who swam with Funghie reported a different experience. So I had to consider the possibility that the source of the beneficial effect of swimming with a dolphin varied with the individual.

The one indisputable fact about the Funghie phenomenon was that almost without exception those who encountered him in free association in his own element – water – were profoundly moved and fell for him. No one has described that personal experience in the open sea more poignantly and powerfully than Heathcote Williams whose long narrative poem and remarkable collection of photographs is fittingly called *Falling for a Dolphin*:

It has approached you, indetectably, from behind.
You suppress an impulse to spin round hastily:
Anxious to see from where, exactly, this apparition came,
Fearing you would take in water through the tube,
And drown.

It draws closer,
Setting no wash.
Staring.
Its grey, telling eye
Inches from yours.

You stare back, startled,
Caught off guard by an intelligence
Both knowing and remote.

With a single movement
It disappears.
As if to allow you to digest the visitation.

Woolly Bear

When the involuntary spurts of adrenalin
Discharged into the surrounding water
Are diluted,
And the shock-waves have ebbed,
It returns
To move up and down your body,
Spraying each section of it with a barrage of echo-
   locating clicks:
Penetrating your brain, heart, lungs, stomach, groin,
   legs and feet;
Seeming to gauge each in depth . . .
Mapping your body's geography
In punctilious detail.

Your brain tingles oddly
As it is spattered, in a second examination,
With unfathomable waves of sound and ultra-sound . . .

The dolphin descends,
Swimming around you, mercurially,
And you pursue it again below.
It whirls and coils,
Describing three-dimensional hieroglyphs in its
   watery space,
Then glances across at you.
A pencil-thin stream of bubbles pours from its blow-hole
As it speaks.
Again, you are lost for a reply,
Immersed in this its element,
Knowing less than nothing.

Above the entrance
Of the oracle of its namesake, Delphi,
Was written the salutary phrase *Gnothee seauton* –
   Know thyself.
And all you know
Is that its serene assurance
Suggests that it knows exactly how to be a dolphin,
And few humans have the foresight to be human.

· 3 ·

Past Lives

The population of most countries in the world has greatly increased over the past 150 years. In consequence, pastoral lands have been transformed beyond recognition. Tracks once used by animals have been covered by concrete, and newly created towns have obliterated all traces of the original native human inhabitants. Today there are no outward signs in Los Angeles or Perth that these cities were once the homelands of American Indians or Australian Aborigines. The way of life and traditions of these former cultures have been smothered by waves of immigrants who came seeking riches and created living styles based upon their new-found wealth.

In stark contrast to this, the population of County Kerry in south-west Ireland has decreased dramatically since 1845 – the first year of the great potato famine, when Ireland had the highest population density in Europe. One result of this decline is that the past has not been swept away. It bubbles up like spring water wherever you turn, and there is no better way of deciphering the past and uncovering the hidden spiritual power of the region than to journey through the Connor Pass towards Slea Head.

Some of the rocks in the mountains that rise around Dingle like the walls of a gargantuan fortress have been scraped and scarred by glacial action. They conjure up visions of a frozen land locked in the grip of the Great Ice Age ten thousand years ago when no humans could have survived here. Exactly how many centuries later they first appeared is not known. The butt of a stone axehead dating from about 3000 BC indicates that the area was inhabited by Stone Age man in Neolithic times. The remains of a fort on the promontory at Dunbeg was once probably a bridge-head of colonisation by the Veneti from Brittany during the Celtic Iron Agewhich began at about 400 BC. Since then no doubt the fort has been modified, partially demolished, and rebuilt many times.

Looking at a map or a chart of the Dingle Peninsula, those with a knowledge of the sea will be aware at once that the waters in Blasket Sound are treacherous for sailors. Innumerable rocks, submerged just below the surface at different states of the tide, lie waiting to set their deadly teeth into any vessel that sails over them, the momentum of ill-fated ships ripping their hulls asunder. The experienced sailor or diver will also deduce from the topography that treacherous currents race through Blasket Sound, hurrying to disaster vessels sailing off course. Even on a calm day, when a spring tide is running fast, white horses charge madly across the blue sea close to the rocks. Put a strong wind against such a tide and the sea boils with a rage and confusion that can have calamitous results, as indeed it did for one of the bedraggled remnants of the Spanish Armada desperately trying to get back home after defeat at the hands of Francis Drake in 1588.

The 160 ships of the mighty Armada must have presented a majestic spectacle when they set out from Spain and sailed into the English Channel. It was the greatest fleet ever assembled. Many of the officers and aristocrats on board took their personal fortunes with them, fully expecting to acquire new estates after the English surrender. But in the event their cumbersome sailing fortresses were put to flight by the smaller and much more nimble English craft that could fire three cannon balls to the Spaniards' one. Surviving vessels of the 'invincible' Armada fled into the North Sea. Their captains hoped to clear the north of Scotland and sail down the west coast of Ireland, home to Spain. Rounding the Shetland Isles the top-heavy galleons met the full force of Atlantic gales, and autumn storms forced them on to the jagged coast of Scotland and Ireland, taking even greater toll than had the English fleet. Thirty ships foundered at sea and another thirty were wrecked on shore.

Captain Juan Martinez of the Spanish galleon *Santa Maria de la Rosa* probably counted himself luckier than most to reach Blasket Sound where two other Spanish ships, the *San Juan de Portugal* and the *San Juan*, were already taking shelter. These vessels were in no better shape than his own and could offer no assistance when desperately he fired his one remaining cannon as a signal for help.

In his book, *Treasure Divers*, Kendall McDonald deduces that the ill-fated *Santa Maria de la Rosa* struck a submerged rock. He also reveals an inaccuracy in the log of the captain of the *San Juan*, who reported that the entire crew of the *Santa Maria de la Rosa* perished on 20 September 1588. One sailor did reach the shore alive. He was taken to Dingle to be interrogated by James Trant, the local agent of Sir Edward Denny. Trant had already questioned other Spaniards, captured when raiding parties came in search of food and fresh water, but it is unlikely that all those who got ashore were taken by the English, or returned to their ships. In due time they doubtless added their own ingredients to the local population.

I do not know if any Spanish survivors settled on Great Blasket itself. Looking at it from the mainland, it is hard to believe that the island once supported a self-sufficient community of more than 200, and that the smaller islands nearby were also permanently inhabited. Of course, in the days before the Industrial Revolution people's expectations were far less in terms of material wealth than they are today. A strong body and a good set of teeth were the main requirements for survival. There were many times when little food was available. During the long dark days of winter the islanders distracted themselves from the pangs of hunger by sitting round their turf fires telling each other stories. With the entire community numbering fewer than a small present-day school, each islander must have known every one of his or her neighbours well. In such a tight society there would be no loneliness, and no need for psychiatrists, although no doubt there would be physical discomfort and hardship. Today, although the Blaskets are occupied during the summer months, the inhabitants are like migrant birds and move away with the approach of winter.

Usually the seasonal settlers arrive at or depart from the tiny harbour of Dunquin, where the jetty is reached by a steep track that zig-zags down from the clifftops to a sheltered flat base and where upturned currachs are arranged as neatly as eggs in a box. Seen from above, these pitch-painted hulls look like a cluster of giant black beetles. Closer inspection reveals that they are constructed of canvas stretched over a framework of wooden slats. At first they appear too frail to be seaworthy, but history proves otherwise. These cockleshell boats were once used to transport people and their livestock across the open sea from the mainland to the Great Blasket, and from island to island. Even the long oars look inadequate. Surely they should have blades on them? Practical use, however, reveals that bladed oars are quite unnecessary to propel these light-weight craft, which are far less exhausting to row than traditional longboats. Watching them skimming across the surface during practice for the Dingle Regatta, I would not be surprised to hear that currachs are the most energy-efficient craft employing muscle power ever devised for transporting humans across water.

Built of simple, readily available materials, the currach reached a pinnacle of design before the Industrial Revolution, and it is still little known outside Ireland. It would be easy for it to be overshadowed in a museum by vessels of more flamboyant design and colour. But set beside white surf, a blue sea, and the flotsam on a beach in the Dingle Peninsula, the black bean-shaped hull of a currach has an aesthetic quality that is not due entirely to its shape and line. It is imbued with the ghosts of the men, women and children of the offshore islands. The currach was an integral part of their lives – a source of many adventures and misadventures. For those forced to leave the Blaskets, never to return, the currach, with its escort of dolphins and porpoises, which

abounded in the area, was their last contact with a community and way of life they would sadly miss.

Many of the cops in present-day New York are the children
and grandchildren of Irish immigrants. It says a lot for the
adaptability of the human race to see how different they are
now, or appear to be, from their forebears and those who
stayed behind in Ireland. But put them in an Irish pub behind
a pint of Guinness and the heritage they carry in their genes
is unleashed like a geyser. Mention 'crack' to an American
and he or she will think you are referring to drugs; yet the
long-established meaning of the same word to every true
Irishman is altogether different. For him 'good crack' can
take as many forms as the clouds in the sky – and, like the
clouds, it cannot be captured and transported elsewhere.
One of its most popular expressions is a story, preferably
romantic, told with any amount of poetic licence provided it
adds to the entertainment of the yarn. Let me offer you some
Irish-style crack . . .

Imagine you are in Dingle in the summer of 1991. The
town is full of visitors, many of whom have come to see
Ireland's now famous friendly wild dolphin. It is late
evening. The air is soft and warm as you make your way
slowly with the crowds idling along the Quay and the
Strand, absorbing the atmosphere of the bars, the restaurants
and the gift shops that are still open. The sound of music and
conversation, muted by windows and walls, tempts you but
you resist until you reach the Holy Ground. Here you find
yourself drawn to O'Flaherty's, its well-worn exterior
blending like heather on a hillside with the rest of the street.
You push open the heavy door and walk into a wall of sound
and thick yellow light. You hesitate for a moment, then
enter. The room is thronged with people, and you squeeze
sideways between them towards the counter. While you
order a drink, a man with a black beard and glittering dark
eyes, who has a university degree in computer studies but
is working the summer as a deckhand on one of the

fishing boats, spots the dolphin printed on your tee-shirt.

'Are you here to see the dolphin?' he inquires.

Having heard that you are, he tells you how the dolphin, or 'your man' as he refers to him, plays around his fishing boat when he's coming into the harbour. He reveals what dolphins have meant to him since he was a boy, and that one of his favourite stories is that of Arion. He reminds you of the myth that Arion was a song-writer and musician who left his home in Lesbos in the Aegean to find fame and fortune. He was said to play the harp more beautifully than any musician in Greece. When he sang of heroes, his voice was manly and vigorous; when he spoke of love, he sang softly to the whispering notes of his lyre. His talent was recognised in Corinth, where he played in King Periander's court and became a great celebrity.

Transfixing you with his eyes, the storyteller moves closer. His intimate tones imply that his next words are for your ears alone. He prepares you for a revelation, but just as he is about to unveil the secret, the babble of conversation around you dips and a group of musicians sitting in a circle on the far side of the room start to play, and another story begins to unfold.

One of the group bows a fiddle. Another, with a double-headed stick that he flicks with rapid twists of his wrists, beats a single-skinned hand-held drum, called a bodhram. The thin rat-a-tat-tat beat conjures images of a drummer leading a platoon of red-coated soldiers through the streets. A girl standing in their midst starts to sing. Her voice rises like a lark over the fiddle and the drum and hovers in the twisting swirls of smoke. The high soprano cuts through the noisy babble of the room which falls like wheat to the blade of a reaper. The powerful notes, crystal clear, penetrate every ear and command every brain to listen. All conversation ceases. The barman stops serving and places a half-filled glass on the bar.

The girl is singing in Irish. Her song tells of the heroic deeds of one of her countrymen during the days of the bitter struggle to throw off the English yoke. It massages the souls of her audience. Some listen with heads bowed, letting the music flow over them like the sea over pebbles. Others, with unblinking eyes, watch; transfixed by the face, the flowing dark hair, the deep-blue eyes and the sounds that pour with the force of a waterfall from her unpainted lips. The drummer bursts into action again as gunfire lays low the defiant hero of her song. The drum and the voice stop abruptly.

There are two seconds of silence. Then the mesmerised audience realise the song is over and burst into applause. The barman finishes pulling his pint, conversations resume, and the room once again floods with the muddy swampwater of sound. The bearded deckhand fixes you again with his glittering eye.

'I think Arion has been reincarnated and is here in Dingle,' he says, joining this thought to his last statement as if the interlude with the Irish singer had not existed. 'Did I not see him myself, sitting on a rock. And was he not playing his harp to the dolphin. Sure, I couldn't believe my eyes.' He scans the pub as if desperately looking for someone to confirm his story. Suddenly his eyes light with delight and surprise.

'That's him, there,' he says, pointing out a young man with loose blonde curls who has appeared in the corner where the girl singer and musicians are gathered.

Your eyes focus on the small twin-horned harp he is carrying. With unconscious self-assurance the new arrival sweeps his fingers across the lyre. The notes from the plucked strings flow across the room like a swallow skimming over a dark pool. Once again all conversation subsides, allowing the musician to carry his audience back in time on an imaginary journey to King Periander's court in Corinth, where a musician called Arion achieved great success before setting sail for the Greek colonies in Sicily and Italy.

The lyrics reveal that the Greeks of old held contests for poets and musicians as well as for athletes. After winning many awards in the Sicilian games Arion amassed a great fortune. Then the musician became homesick and chartered a Corinthian vessel to take him back to Lesbos. He embarked at Taras, at the foot of Italy. The crew watched Arion's possessions coming aboard and were envious. Once out to sea, they plotted to kill him and make off with his treasure. But it is difficult to keep a secret like that on a small boat. When Arion learned of the plan, he begged for his life. The crew refused, realising that, if he told King Periander, they themselves would be doomed. They did, however, concede to one of Arion's requests – that he should sing to them before they put him to death. So, dressed in his finest clothes, Arion sang a high-pitched song to one of the gods.

His song-prayer was answered in the form of a dolphin that gambolled alongside, whereupon Arion surprised his would-be killers by jumping overboard. He climbed on to the head of the dolphin and was ferried to the shore at Tainaron. As a votive offering to the gods for his rescue Arion commissioned a statue of himself riding on a dolphin and had it placed in the temple at Cape Tainaron.

The musician concludes by saying that if anyone doubts his song they should refer to the works of the Greek historian Herodotus who saw the statue in the temple and was so intrigued that he unearthed the story of how it got there. His account, written in 450 BC, is now enshrined in ancient Greek literature.

'Was that really Arion reincarnated and telling his own story?' you ask yourself.

You turn to the deckhand in the hope that he will expand on his proposal. But he has gone. You decide to ask the man who sang the song, but he too has disappeared. You push your way to the door and join the animated crowd still wandering past. The fresh air clears your head a little. You dawdle as aimlessly as everyone else to wherever your feet carry you, wandering. Wondering if the man who sang the song really was telling his own story of a past life.

· 4 ·

I'll Be Watching You

The story of Arion has lodged in my memory since childhood. Having seen my young son Ashley spontaneously given a ride by a friendly free dolphin off the coast of the Isle of Man in 1974, I would be surprised if there were not a valid basis for the tale which originated some 2,500 years ago. Arion certainly could have met a friendly dolphin and perhaps even been carried on one. But was his more likely to be an elaborate metaphor for a rescue of another kind – a deeply emotional one? After all Arion was a romantic songwriter as well as a singer, and as such would be entitled to use what we now call poetic licence. An event in London on 26 October 1991 caused me to ponder on this possibility.

The reason for my presence in London was to make a contribution to the first Whale and Dolphin Conservation Society conference. The brainchild of Sean Whyte, the event took place at London University's Logan Hall where the 930 seats were filled to overflowing and renowned speakers gathered to relate their experiences with cetaceans and the problems that faced them. Among them was Dr Paul Spong, who had travelled from Hanson Island, Vancouver, in British Colombia to tell an enraptured audience about his remarkable work at Orcalab with the largest of the dolphins, *Orcinus orca*, the Killer whale.

Many of those present were in tears while he described how, in studies that spanned two decades, he had started to unravel the social life of the huge dolphins which arrived every summer to spend time in the waters outside his home and workplace. Cameras and an array of underwater microphones, called hydrophones, provided him with the visual and sound images from which he pieced together the remarkable life histories of a group of animals whose common name, Killer whales, belied their true characters. His painstaking research revealed that there were lifelong bonds between family members. Far from being ruthless killers, he reported that the tribes, or pods, close to whose summer feeding ground he happened to have set up his own residence, had gentle harmonious relationships with virtually all of the other animals they encountered – apart, of course, from the fish which they took as food. Their passivity even extended to the so-called transients – other Killer whales, with a reputation for hunting and eating mammals such as seals, dolphins, and even the large baleen whales, that moved freely through the area at irregular and widely-spaced intervals. The resident pods allowed such visitors passage, without much contact and without hindrance. The local groups certainly did not exhibit the same territorial displays of aggression that are characteristic of virtually all other living creatures – especially man.

Dr Spong attributed this tolerance to a unique and total absence of fear. He pointed out that man's presence on the planet was a mere blip in the time of twenty million years or more that the Killer whales had occupied the oceans. Arguably they had evolved during their long history to become the supreme beings on the planet. Fear was not necessary for the survival of such a species. The dolphins, Dr Spong implied, were ahead of humans in evolutionary terms.

'Can you imagine what life would be like if humans had no fear of one another?' he asked rhetorically, pressing home the point.

In a personal profile on him in the Summer 1987 issue of *Whalewatcher*, the journal of The American Cetacean Society, Patricia Warhol posed the question of whether or not Paul Spong was a prophet, which Webster's dictionary defines as: *One gifted with more than ordinary spiritual and moral insight.*

My own introduction to Paul Spong's work came in 1976

45

when I was presented with a copy of *Mind in the Waters* – a collection of writings assembled by Joan McIntyre which would help to change public consciousness. It is a book I cherish, one that has had a profound effect on me. 'The Whale Now', Spong's contribution to the book, is an autobiographical account of how he, a psychologist from New Zealand, was greatly changed when he started working with an Orca named Skana in the Vancouver Public Aquarium in 1969. Contemplation of the results of his 1970 programme led Spong to conclude that he was too pre-occupied with the technical aspects of his work and had not paid enough attention to the whales themselves. So, in 1971, he started using a one-man kayak to interface with Orcas swimming freely in the open sea. He described the emotional impact of his new-style, open-water research thus:

> During these first kayak excursions with free Orcas, I was frequently thrilled by moments of joyous interaction between myself and the whales . . . These were wonderful, ecstatic days in which I experienced a feeling for and closeness to the creatures that will ever remain with me.

One such day was 11 August 1971, which began with a heavy fog hanging over Hanson Island. Dr Spong decided to go out briefly in his kayak, taking only his flute and leaving behind his compass, chart, food and water. Through the fog he heard the sound of the Killer whales, or Orcas. He put down his paddle, picked up his flute and, with eyes closed, started to play. When he opened them again, Paul was aware that there were Orcas all around him in the fringes of the fog. He estimated more than fifty of them, and when they started to move off, he paddled after them. It seemed clear to the scientist that the whales wanted him to follow, but which group should he pursue? He decided on the one with the most babies. When they disappeared, he headed for a group of eight older juveniles and young adult males. He became so excited when they swam in line abreast, four on each side of him, that he tried to touch them, nearly overbalancing his kayak in the process. He felt a bit foolish when they immediately disappeared, so he played his flute again, and they all came back, making passes as close as ten feet. The enchanted flautist lost all sense of time and became lost in the mist. He landed on the first island that loomed out of the fog, waited for it to disperse, and then headed back home. In all the trip lasted ten hours.

After that Paul Spong often played music to the whales, which would hover offshore, apparently tuning in to the man-made sounds. Still nights were particularly rewarding. Sometimes the Orcas seemed to join the celebration with a chorus of their own voices and the dance of their bodies, which were visible from the bubbling phosphorescent wakes they left in the black water.

In more than twenty years of study Spong witnessed a few minor disagreements but never saw Orcas fighting one another. 'The pods are structured, and we think they are matriarchal. But the question of pod leadership is mysterious because of the absence of aggression. In most species, including ours, we see struggles for dominance, and the most aggressive or the most powerful wins and becomes leader. But we haven't observed that behaviour in Orcas. I don't know what regulations they have, but something works.'

If the apparent absence of leadership and dominant hierarchy still puzzled him, Dr Spong was quite clear about the importance of family in an Orca's daily life. 'Killer whales live in close family groups; they're born into a family, live their lives within it and die within it. Their lives are focused around the reality of the pod – caring for the young, feeding. They lead a peaceful co-operative existence,' he told the meeting.

Having made this point gently but forcefully, Paul Spong went on with a quiet but passionate plea on behalf of Corky, a female Orca who had been incarcerated since her capture in Pender Harbour in 1969. During her stay in captivity all six of the babies to which she had given birth had died. By 1991 she had ceased to ovulate and was, according to the dolphinarium authorities, near to the end of her life. Spong maintained that had she remained in the wild, with a life expectancy of 70 years, Corky would be in her prime. Furthermore she would still be part of the family group, Top Notch's pod, from which she had been ignominiously and involuntarily plucked.

After spending almost all her life imprisoned in a tiny pool, entertaining hundreds of thousands of dollar-paying customers while rapidly approaching a premature death, surely Corky was entitled to spend the rest of her days in the company of her family. Spong knew who Corky's relatives were and when they frequented Vancouver, and that the pod would welcome Corky back if given the opportunity. All that remained, therefore, was to get Sea World in San Diego to release Corky and mobilise the resources needed to give her back her dignity and her freedom.

Unfortunately Anheuser-Busch, the company that owned Budweiser Beer, as well as Sea World, didn't see the situation in the same light. Despite their tacit agreement at first, the company had since taken a strong stance against the return of the performing Killer whale to her natural environment. It was now a race against time. Would the weeks, months, years it had taken to resolve the wrangle over her future exceed her foreshortened lifespan? The outcome was uncertain, but the issue was clear enough, and in some respects it was similar to that of slavery.

To my mind the outcome was inevitable. Killer whales would eventually cease to be captured and put on public display, but how long the war would last I could not tell.

I had met Paul Spong for the first time the night before his presentation. With us was another person I had not seen before. Debbie Jamison had breezed into our hotel dressed in a black hat and clothes that set her apart as a young lady of style and artistic flair. Her deep brown eyes, almost black in the dim light, glowed like just-ignited fireworks. They conveyed the feeling that she relished life and was poised for the moment when she would burst forth and add her own brilliant sparkle to the proceedings. Anyone might have assumed she was a successful, self-confident career woman who hadn't a care in the world. At that moment she probably was, but I knew that this had not always been the case, for a few weeks earlier she had written to tell me how she had come to hear of my 'Operation Sunflower' experiment and the dolphin experience that had changed her life. Here is part of what she wrote:

I have had various emotionally related problems in the past and have always been a deeply sensitive person. But just under two years ago, at the age of 20, I was suffering from a deep depression that I could not seem to get myself out of. It was an awful time, not only for me but for friends and family also. I was desperately unhappy and getting to the end of my tether. It occurred to me more than once to end my life, though I never went as far as putting that thought into action.

By chance I had a leaflet with Poppie Adam's phone number on it. To my delight, she told me about Freddie the Amble dolphin. I was elated (as much as I could be given my circumstances). A week after my conversation with Poppie, pale and drawn, I arrived in Amble.

Twenty minutes later I was entering Freddie's world wearing a much too thin borrowed wet-suit, in far from calm seas. I was freezing but this did not deter me. He arrived straight away and circled me. Then he came up and looked me straight in the eyes as he swam past – I felt that he was looking directly into my soul. I must have passed the test because he then appeared offering me his white stomach to be rubbed. My first experience with this wonderful creature was totally timeless and free of any limitations. For the first time in ages I was smiling and laughing from the bottom of my heart. Freddie had accepted and loved me for no other reason than that he wanted to, no strings attached. When I left the water I was numb, ecstatic, tears of love and joy ran down my face. I was worth something, I finally mattered, not just to Freddie but to myself. I cannot describe my experience of swimming with a dolphin totally in words, but it is not just a physical or mental experience. It is spiritual and magical. They have so much that they could teach us about harmony, unconditional love and the spiritual side of life that we often ignore.

I am now totally recovered, and better than ever before. I have taken Freddie's magic into my everyday life. I am a much calmer, loving and tolerant person. Also my creativity has expanded amazingly (I am a singer, songwriter). I have been to see Freddie a lot since that first encounter, and have just returned from a wonderful two weeks in Amble. I am so lucky that he is my friend.

From her letter it was apparent that, with little previous knowledge of the work I had done with dolphins and people suffering from depression, Debbie had stumbled on the idea that meeting a dolphin would help her through an emotional crisis. Her intuition was right. For her it had certainly worked. Debbie's meetings with Freddie, the dolphin in Amble, had restored her to her former cheerful self, and my contribution to the conference reflected my deep personal interest in the effect of dolphins on the human psyche. I was still trying to identify precisely what it was that gave dolphins their special magic, and my presence in London provided an opportunity to meet Debbie. Could this articulate young woman give me the vital clue I was looking for?

As it turned out the gathering in London, with all the excitement and tension of an imminent conference, was not a suitable time to explore the chain of events that had led to her taking the action she did. Our frequently interrupted conversation did not reveal a neat and simple explanation. On the train journey home, however, when I was reflecting on what she had said, the fact that she was a songwriter and singer reminded me that 2,500 years earlier Arion was, as it were, in the same kind of business. And that caused me to ask myself what really happened in ancient Greece.

Casually I picked up a discarded newspaper in the carriage and read that the singer Sting wrote the song *I'll Be Watching*

You after the break-up of his marriage. Immediately the melody and lyrics of his song ran through my mind. When I had first heard them, I did not know the circumstances in which they were written, but the hurt he was feeling was all too apparent.

A high percentage of popular ballads are written around personal experience. It is a prerequisite for lyricists to be highly sensitive. Sometimes the truth is there for all to see or hear. More often, however, it is disguised, and only those close to the lyricist know the source of his or her inspiration.

As the train rattled through the night thoughts of Arion in the court of King Periander washed in and out of my mind like waves lapping the shore. Were the ancient Greeks, consciously or subconsciously, aware of what I had observed, namely that dolphins can help people through periods of heartbreak and mental ill health? Was that why the ancient Greeks held that to kill a dolphin was a crime punishable by death? If so, had the reason for Arion's departure from Corinth been a broken heart, and were the songs he wrote and the statue he later commissioned his way of expressing his special thanks to the dolphins for helping him through a deep emotional crisis?

Neither I nor anyone else could answer these questions, but asking them helped to pass the journey.

When finally I got into my car in the early hours of the morning to complete the final leg of my journey home, I knew that I would watch with interest the future career of Debbie Jamison, who was still very young. I speculated on how pleased I would be at some future date to learn that she had made it into the charts with a song conveying her feelings, directly or indirectly, about Freddie the Amble dolphin. If she did hit the big time, Debbie would not be the first to be inspired by dolphins and subsequently achieve success. The internationally renowned songwriter and singer Willy M, whose first physical contact with a dolphin was also at Amble, had done that already with his group Londonbeat.

· 5 ·

A Threat to Freddie

Visitors arriving in Amble are greeted by bold road signs proclaiming they are entering THE FRIENDLIEST PORT. This is not a misleading epithet. Yet those expecting the road to lead down to a picturesque harbour, bordered by pastel-painted houses adorned with geranium-filled window boxes, and with a jetty extending a curved arm into the sea, will have their romantic illusions quickly shattered. There is nothing frivolous or soft about Amble. Its inner streets proclaim its heritage – a working town where life was tough, and for most inhabitants it still is. Almost all the old houses have doors opening directly on to the pavement. The main shopping thoroughfare, Queen Street, is functionally straight and its eastern end is dominated by a Co-op supermarket whose windows are plastered with gaudy stickers. The small harbour beside the Lifeboat Station is rectangular and overlooked by a car park.

Pictures in a local guidebook graphically capture the essence of Amble in former years when, besides fishing, coal-shipping was the main activity in the harbour. An aerial photograph taken in 1969 reveals that the harbour was caught between the horns of two overhead railway lines that carried coal wagons to colliers moored along the dockside. Completing the final leg of their journey under gravity the wagons would run down to a staithe where a man called a teemer would hammer out the chock which locked a hinged flap at the bottom of the truck. The released coal would then thunder down a chute into the hold of a ship where it was shovelled by a team of trimmers to ensure the load was evenly spread. The work of these men was hard and danger-ous. They laboured in the dust and darkness, sometimes with only a candle for light. Above them teemers manually moved the remainder of the coal in the wagons into the chutes. Every teemer's ambition was to become a trimmer because they were better paid and self-employed.

During its life as a coal port Amble was a dirty place. Even the colliers were coal-fired, adding their smoke to that which belched out from the steam engines that hauled the goods trains and spewed from the dock-side brickworks. Gordon Easton, the present-day mechanic of the lifeboat, told me wryly that he could remember the time when ships' crews put on their working clothes before coming ashore for a night out in Amble.

Jim and Brenda Henderson, the proprietors of the Harbour Guest House, had no regrets about the passing of the 'hard old days'. Jim was born in 1939 and lived with his parents in a rent-free colliery house which had no electricity or running water. His father kept a spittoon beside his bed and a po under it. The outside lavatory, across the dirt street, consisted of a wooden bench with a hole in it, over a pit. The luxury of toilet paper was unknown. Squares of old news-paper, tied with a piece of string to a nail hammered into the door, were used for wiping bottoms. The contents of the pit, along with ash from the household fires, were removed once a week by a man who, Jim told me with some pride, had never missed a day's work in his life.

Down the pit Jim rose to the rank of 'roper', which involved setting-up and maintaining the many cables used underground. He often worked far out under the sea. Despite the pumps, which laboured night and day to remove water, the tunnels in which he struggled with steel hawsers were often flooded with up to four feet of black water. Before there were pithead baths he would wash away the grime in a galvanised tub with water heated on the kitchen range. His mother, and later his wife, would wash his work clothes daily. He had only one set that had to be dried immediately in front of the open fire in time for his next shift. When the last of the houses was demolished in 1972, Jim and Brenda had moved to a council house in Amble which, by comparison, was luxurious accommodation.

At eleven years old, Jim was given the task of running to one of his aunts and telling her that her husband had been killed down the mine. Later he witnessed many accidents, some due to the sacrifice of safety for higher productivity. Having to put someone's brains into a bag when a stanchion collapsed and crushed a man's skull was one of the memories he would like to expunge, but cannot. Jim openly admits that no mine can be completely safe, and, like all pit workers, he enjoyed the comradeship of his fellows. When Hawksley Colliery was closed in 1987, he took voluntary redundancy and used the money to move from coal mining to hotel management.

The use of such high-flown words to describe the running of their guest house, from peeling potatoes to cleaning the loos, would, I am sure, bring an uninhibited smile to Brenda's face. For the famous Geordie sense of humour quickly finds a way of turning into a joke the fact that she knows only too well the reality of her situation. Brenda radiates a generosity and resilience of spirit which stems from her roots in a community where tough times were the norm and survival depended upon neighbours helping one another.

When Brenda and Jim first took over the Harbour Guest House they catered mainly for fishing parties, holidaymakers and peripatetic workers and technicians. In short, the kind of people they expected. The arrival of a dolphin shortly afterwards resulted in an altogether unexpected clientele. People of all shapes and sizes, from various walks of life and from many different parts of the world, came knocking at their door. They arrived seeking spiritual ecstasy, fulfilment of deep-felt desires, relief from mental stress, in search of wisdom, networking, looking for photo opportunities and for a host of other reasons that did not fall into the normal experience of a couple from the Hendersons' background.

I first heard about the dolphin from Richard Edwards,

a local TV cameraman who specialised in underwater photography. But it was a later letter from Paul Spies in London which alerted me to the pleasures of the Harbour Guest House. He also provided me with a graphic description of his own experiences with the friendly dolphin, which at the time was called Dougal by several of those who swam with him, plus a map and a photograph, all of which were published in the International Dolphin Watch journal of December 1988.

I arrived at Amble on 12th November 1988 and immediately made my way to the end of the pier at the harbour entrance where a dolphin is reputed to live. After a wait of about half an hour a dorsal fin appeared alongside an incoming fishing boat. A large Bottlenose dolphin of about 12–13 feet in length rolled gracefully under and around the vessel. For about an hour and a half I watched him (or is he a she – I never saw his/her underside close enough to tell) as he dived and surfaced anywhere between the large buoy and the harbour entrance. The local fisherman told me that he liked the buoy because of the sound its chain made when rattled by the currents. As with all dolphins he was extremely difficult to photograph at short range as he was never in one place for more than five seconds.

I had arranged with one of the villagers to take me out in his boat and at 2 p.m. we passed the two beacons on the piers that mark the opening to the harbour. Soon the now familiar dorsal fin joined us and the dolphin dived under and around the boat. He darted everywhere and it was extremely difficult to know where he would pop up next. While this was going on an inflatable was being launched and soon arrived with three divers on board – they were being escorted by you-know-who at the bow.

After getting into my wetsuit I jumped over the side of our boat to join the divers who were now swimming with the dolphin. He soon came over to me and watched me very intently under water. Unfortunately I couldn't enter wholeheartedly into the exciting mood as my face was burning from the cold. What I did see (not very much as the water was very murky and I am short sighted into the bargain) was a beautiful smiling dolphin's face gently poised about a metre from mine. We both looked each other in the eye for a few moments until I could bear the cold no longer. It is always so exciting when first coming into close contact with a dolphin and that day was no exception.

I saw him on Sunday as well, but when in the water could not entice him into the harbour entrance where I was freezing from the cold whilst tapping two stones together below the surface. I also saw him playing with a large salmon of about forty centimetres in length. He threw it up into the air several times, catching it again when it hit the water. At one stage he also rolled over on his back and just lay on the surface. He enjoyed the boats but would not spend too long with them. He seemed to have a fixed territory for most of the time between the lighthouse beacons and the large buoy, tending to come closer to the harbour entrance at high tide when the fish were probably closer inshore.

I had a wonderful weekend and was looked after extremely well by Mrs Henderson at the Harbour Guest House, which is situated five minutes away from all the excitement . . .

Despite Paul's references to the searing cold of the North Sea it was not long before a stream of dolphin watchers, myself among them, arrived in Amble to taste the delights of swimming with a friendly wild dolphin which chose to make his home base over a sewage outfall that served, in addition to Amble, the town of Morpeth some twelve miles away. Undeterred by the foreign objects that emerged from the undersea pipe, the number of people jumping into the sea to swim with Dougal, or Freddie, as subsequently he became better known, steadily increased.

When Freddie took up residence off Amble, it became feasible for many people, especially those in Britain with limited financial resources, to enjoy the magic of seeing and swimming with a dolphin in open water, despite the chilly North Sea. But for many the opportunity almost vanished when suddenly Freddie's life was put in jeopardy. On Saturday, 22 December 1989, an unexploded mine was hauled up in a fishing net and dumped in the middle of Freddie's adopted territory off the Amble harbour mouth.

One of the first to hear about the mine was Tricia Kirkman, who received a telephone call from Brenda Henderson. It was Tricia's super-sensitive response to Percy, the dolphin off the coast of Cornwall, and later her close relationship with Simo in South Wales, that were directly responsible for me setting up Operation Sunflower. During the making of the film *Bewitched by a Dolphin* I uncovered some of the dramatic and traumatic events that had shaped her life. It was her announcement that Percy gave her 'unconditional love' that set me on a quest to find out just what could cause such a profound and positive change of mood in people, especially those, like Tricia, who suffered from severe attacks of anxiety.

As a result of her dolphin encounters Tricia certainly was a changed woman. Even so, her basic personality remained the same. 'Nothing in moderation' was her motto. In the spring of 1989 she moved into a derelict house, which she immediately started to restore, and changed her name to Poppie Adam – both typical of her impulsive nature. Her passion for dolphins remained, and she took advantage of whatever opportunities came her way to visit Freddie.

Tricia (alias Poppie) knew how curious Freddie was about virtually any diver who visited his territory, especially one engaged in mechanical tasks underwater. When she heard that a Royal Navy team had been called in to detonate the mine, she flew headlong into panic stations. Into her mind sprang an image of Freddie intently watching the divers fixing their detonation charges to the mine and then staying nearby when they hastily retreated from the burning fuse. The notion of Freddie being blown to smithereens when the mine exploded was simply unbearable for her.

She tried to telephone me, but I was on my way to Scotland to give a lecture. Then frantically she started to telephone every person she could think of who might intercede to stop the mine being exploded. These included Greenpeace International, the Amble police, the Secretary of International Dolphin Watch (whom she got out of bed at 2.30 in the morning) and Owen Davies. He immediately packed his diving gear into his car and set off at dead of night for Amble, so that he could be on the spot to confront the divers when they arrived the following morning. Owen himself was intensely involved with Freddie, and indeed had taken part in a programme in Welsh for television in which he explained how swimming with dolphins had enabled him to overcome some of his own emotional problems.

Owen had a droll sense of humour, but his curly black hair and dark eyes were hints to his Celtic roots. One of the causes of his mental stress was that he would latch on to catastrophic situations and brood on them. When he was angry, black light shone from his eyes. Owen was short, passionate and immensely strong physically. He was not a man to be crossed. He was just the person to represent Tricia in Amble. Like her, if other protests failed, he would have tied himself to the mine to prevent it being exploded when Freddie the dolphin was nearby.

While Owen drove through the night in freezing fog, Tricia, who was ill with the 'flu, continued her frenetic campaign to save Freddie. Making full use of her bedside telephone, she contacted some of the many people she knew in the media as early as possible the next morning.

No diver in the world would deliberately destroy a dolphin, and the Naval demolition team enjoyed diving with Freddie as much as anyone else. Besides, those in authority in the Admiralty knew that if the Royal Navy accidentally killed or seriously injured Freddie there would be a tremendous public outcry, especially as the media, having been alerted by Tricia, were turning up in force in Amble.

To his surprise, Owen found a sympathetic reception awaiting him. He was assured that his concern for the well-being of the dolphin was shared by all those involved. The detonation of the mine was put on hold until a plan was contrived that would ensure the safety of the dolphin. Eventually it was agreed that Owen would swim with Freddie while the charges were laid. Just before the mine was exploded he would entice the dolphin behind the break-water.

The plan worked. In the water Owen felt a dull thud when the explosion took place. Freddie, who must also have felt it, showed no obvious signs of distress and continued to frolic. Owen was later presented with a special award by the RSPCA for his prompt and effective action to save Freddie.

· 6 ·

Three Musketeers and Sky's the Limit

The threat to Freddie's life by a left-over mine from the Second World War made many more people aware of the presence of a friendly dolphin in Amble and they arrived in ever-increasing numbers to see for themselves. The chance to swim with a dolphin, expenses paid, was an opportunity not to be missed by those in the media who could convince their editors that they would come back with a good story. Reports of the terror on jumping into the cold North Sea in the presence of a 12-foot monster, and then the thrill and joy of being in the water when Freddie gently rolled over to have his belly stroked, appeared in many newspapers alongside pictures of intrepid reporters cavorting with a dolphin.

I accompanied several of them, and was pleased to do so, for here were, if you like, professional observers looking objectively at a situation in which I openly admitted I was involved at many levels. I wanted to find out how their observations and conclusions matched-up or conflicted with my own.

Hugo Davenport ended his report for the *Weekend Telegraph* (25 August 1990) as follows:

> Among the swimmers on the day of my visit, reactions are varied. Television director Jim Cellan Jones: 'He's like a great puppy, but you do get an eerie feeling of great intelligence.' Pop singer Willy M, of Londonbeat: 'I am not really into spiritual, mystical things at all, but this is spiritual and mystical.' BBC presenter Valerie Singleton: 'What I felt from Freddie, most of all, was irritation.'

For my own part, wearing only half a wetsuit and freezing cold, it was still the realisation of a childhood dream. I could not swear, as some do, that the dolphin showed me 'pure love', but I shall not soon forget that quizzical eye, with its unaccountable suggestion of humour.

A two-page colour feature in the *Independent on Sunday* (26 August 1990) appeared under the headline 'Flipper Was Never Like This'. The by-line went: '*Lynne Truss defies her fear of the deep to test a theory that dolphins can help cure depression.*' Lynne described Freddie 'eerily magnified' in the water as she floated round the boat, peering down at the dolphin beneath her.

> . . . Occasionally he would surface for air alongside us. I remember making oh-my-goodness noises through my snorkel, but otherwise the lasting impression of my face-to-face was that it happened in total silence.
>
> Hauled back aboard, I felt an enormous pleasure in what had occurred. Was this something to do with the dolphin's special aura? As we headed back to Amble for our breakfast I tried to be analytical, and tell myself I was just proud of my measly act of courage or infatuated with the improbable idea of myself as a wetsuited James Bond girl; but there was no denying I felt fantastically good.

Earlier in her piece Lynne Truss examined what I had said in my book, *Dance to a Dolphin's Song*, about contact with a dolphin being akin to a religious experience for some people.

> I can verify one strand of this analogy, which is that when people undergo a religious conversion, all their friends feel uncomfortable and hope it will soon pass, ('Still going on about dolphins is she?'). But without being blasphemous isn't there something obviously religious – and specifically Christian – about the symbolism of dolphins? They visit from another world; they bring joy by loving mankind unjudgementally; despite their superior strength, they are never aggressive towards people, even when suffering; and they die because of man's stupidity and greed.

Chris Salewicz, who wrote an article entitled 'Soothing love from a hermit of the sea' for the *Sunday Correspondent*, was in Amble when I was there making a short film for Channel 4 with three children who suffered from cerebral palsy. We had a full television film crew, and as well as being an adventure with a dolphin, it was for the youngsters an exciting experience of performing before camera. The eldest, Vicky Bell, age 14, had very limited mobility and was confined to a wheelchair. She was unable to go into the water, so the storyline concentrated on Simon Grey, age 11, and Althea Edwards, age 12. I referred to them as 'The Three Musketeers' because they all knew one another and there was a great deal of camaraderie, especially between Simon and Althea who were obviously very close friends. Despite the hazards, the dangers and their disabilities, meeting Freddie was for them a glorious romp.

When Simon and Althea got into the water in their wetsuits, the cold hit them like a mallet. After a few minutes another boatload of dolphin seekers arrived. As soon as one of them entered the water Freddie left us and stayed with her. Our two young aquatic performers weren't disconcerted. They had done their bit and were only too glad not to be pushed by a zealous film director into staying in the cold any longer. As I watched I became aware that the woman who now had Freddie's undivided attention was engaged in an intensely emotional experience.

I learned later from Robert Barnes, who had arranged the trip for the newly founded Friends of the Dolphins, that Freddie had released emotional pains this woman had held back for a long time. She had been unable to talk about them before, but she wept for hours after meeting the dolphin. Her tears were not of pain but of relief and joy. I wondered if they contained endomorphines, or endorphins, which are produced naturally in our bodies and make us feel high. Sometimes these substances concentrate in tears, by which they can be excreted. Here at least was a biochemical explanation for the effect even if it did not account for how it was that Freddie could stimulate their release into the brain.

Shortly before Simon and Althea's Freddie experience, which occurred on 15 August 1990, I had gone to see the Oscar-winning film *My Left Foot*. It told the story of the Irish working-class writer and painter who was born paralysed and was dismissed by all except his family. Brown had educated himself. Using only his left foot, he wrote a bestseller and emerged as a renowned painter. Daniel Day Lewis won the award of Best Actor for depicting Christy Brown's conflicting moods, and for conveying to the audience the intelligence and creative energy that burned inside his unco-operative body. What came across to me was the utter frustration he felt when he could not articulate his feelings or the words that swirled round like a whirlpool inside his head.

The two stars of our little film certainly had no need of dolphin therapy. They were imbued with a determination to overcome their disabilities. A joyful, irrepressible spirit radiated from their eyes and showed in their behaviour. Indeed, they were like a couple of dolphins themselves and were happy despite their inability to do all the physical things their unafflicted contemporaries could do. For his part, Freddie greeted them, but then concentrated on the person who had submitted herself totally to him and was in far greater need of his attention than the two children.

Why was it, I asked myself, that those who were suffering emotionally got preferential treatment from Freddie? How and why did he select the people he chose to spend so much more time with than others? There was no doubt from all the evidence that dolphins which sought human company could somehow identify, almost immediately, traits of personality that were sensitive and vulnerable. There was, however, another aspect to the behaviour of those selected for special attention. I had casually observed it before, but did not pinpoint its significance until after I recorded Bill Bowell's first encounters with Freddie. These occasions were also memorable for another unrelated reason – Freddie gave me a black eye. It all happened when once again I was on a filming expedition.

We had agreed to assemble at the Lifeboat Station on 11 July with Eileen Marino and a film crew from TV-AM. Gordon Easton's boat was quickly loaded and soon we were heading down river towards the open sea. We had gone only a short distance before we found Freddie with a member of International Dolphin Watch who had swum out from the end of the pier.

The dolphin obviously liked her company and spent most of his time with her, hooking his penis behind her leg and towing her along, despite the counter-attractions of several other people in the water. It was approaching high water and the conditions were extremely good. Eventually Eileen Marino got in the water and so did I, but Freddie paid us little attention. Once the girl from London had left the scene, Bill flopped into the sea with a small egg-shaped rattle which he shook. Freddie was mesmerised and spent the next half-hour exclusively in Bill's company, despite the presence of myself and several others in the water.

While I was swimming around, a young woman dog-paddled up to me and asked if I were Horace Dobbs – to which, of course, I replied that I was. She had a slight Canadian accent, and I noticed that she was wearing crystal earrings. There was an intense expression about her, almost a haunted look. Freddie came over and greeted her, and then went back to swimming with Bill.

While we were being ignored I couldn't help appreciating how Bill submitted himself to the dolphin and never tried to force the relationship. If Freddie swam away, Bill did not – as almost everyone else did – go swimming frantically after the dolphin. He remained in the same place, making his signal – on this occasion with the egg rattle, previously in Ireland by clicking his fingers – until the dolphin returned, which inevitably it did. I concluded that it was Bill's attitude of mind, as well as his other qualities, which resulted in his preferential treatment.

I also made another observation, which was important for underwater filming. I noticed that the water was considerably clearer as the tide fell (immediately after high tide) than

5 Sunset at Amble

6 Freddie hovers upside down to be stroked by pop star
Willy M of Londonbeat – one of the dolphin's many fans

7 Beata with Freddie

it had been when first we arrived. This, Gordon explained, was due to the tide rising from the south; in other words, over the sewage outfall. When the tide started to fall, the current changed direction and the relatively clear water flowed from the north.

Conditions were perfect after Bill had finished his swim. I was reluctant to join him in the boat because I was captivated by Freddie and the dolphin clearly did not want me to leave. Half in and half out of the water, I clung on to the wooden ladder that hung over the side of the boat while Freddie scratched himself against the stiff tip of one of my submerged fins. Jerking his head vigorously, he made the plastic blade rub his face, under his chin, over the top of his head and around his eye. He had a look of sheer bliss, indicating yet again that he was extremely sensual and sensitive to touch. The sun streaming through the water created waves of golden light that danced over his head and the bright red legs of my wetsuit. Even as I watched, mesmerised by the flickering patterns, I knew that I would cherish memories of this simple touching incident.

The following day the crew were late for our ten o'clock rendezvous. The time for low water was fast approaching. When Bill's wife, Edna, stood on the edge of the jetty and looked down, she was horrified to see the boat so far below her. She had to pluck up all her courage to climb down the slippery iron ladder which was attached to the harbour wall. I had to act as grips to help get all the filming equipment down to the boat before it grounded. The assortment of bags, boxes, cameras and tripods was lowered by rope on to the deck of the lifeboat and then transferred across as quickly as possible to Gordon's boat moored alongside. At about half-past ten we moved away just as the keel of the *G. Jennifer* started to touch bottom. If we had delayed three minutes longer we would have been stuck on the mud.

We were promised a region of high pressure over the British Isles and a day of hot cloudless weather with no wind. Gordon explained that the low water would prevent fishing boats and other keeled vessels from leaving the harbour and the marina. We could expect a spell lasting an hour or so during which there would be little boating activity.

Gordon's forecast turned out to be more accurate than that of the weathermen. There was virtually no traffic and the dolphin came to us as soon as we left the harbour mouth. It was now slack water. With no current and the engine turned off we just drifted, pushed by what little wind there was. The underwater visibility was poor and the fresh water coming down the river made it hazy. Even so Freddie's antics and movements could be clearly seen from the boat. Although the day was grey the dolphin's smile more than made up for the lack of sunlight.

I had stayed the night at one of Brenda Henderson's recommended overflows – The Hellenic Guest House. Unknown to me, the girl with the Canadian accent was also in the same accommodation, and we were both surprised when we met in the dining room for breakfast. She introduced herself as Beata Pillach and told me she had just spent six months modelling in Japan, where she could not accept the hypocrisy that allowed whales killed for scientific research to end up as steaks in restaurants. She had a profound dislike of her father's brutality. When she was 15 years old, she had confronted him, taking off her glasses and inviting him to smack her across the face instead of her mother. Her parents were Polish and she had inherited the passion of her race. Her limbs were pencil thin. From what she said it seemed she lived in a confusing world of emotional extremes.

Beata said how much meeting the dolphin meant to her. Yet in her first encounter Freddie seemed almost to ignore her. She also mentioned the fact that she could not swim, and that it was the first time she had worn fins. She had purchased the fins in London and they were far too tight. I knew from experience they would be agonising to wear, and so I loaned her a pair of orange fins which were somewhat too big for her. To make them fit better, she encased her feet in plastic bags before putting them on.

When eventually she got into the water, the dolphin became progressively more engrossed with her. It was apparent to any onlooker that she was becoming totally absorbed, oblivious to everything and everyone except Freddie with whom her relationship was heightening by the minute. Although Beata couldn't swim, she was very buoyant and started frolicking with the dolphin, talking to him continuously as if she were playing with a schoolfriend. I watched, not attempting to interfere.

At breakfast Beata had said that the dolphin had taught her not to be too grasping. Now he was giving her a second lesson – that once she let go of her inhibitions and fears he would share himself with her. Indeed, Freddie had already taken charge of the situation and was deliberately pushing Beata away from the boat, or so it appeared to me. I called to her not to go too far away, but my advice fell on deaf ears.

Gradually their game became more intense as their relationship developed at an explosive rate. I heard a shriek and looked across to see Beata being propelled rapidly backwards through the water with the dolphin pushing hard against her feet. Faster and faster they went as Freddie became more excited.

Meanwhile Gordon had been trying to position the boat so that Eileen Marino could do a piece to camera with the dolphin frolicking in the background. The wind, the current and the dolphin's frenetic activity all served to thwart him as repeatedly he started the engine, manoeuvred a little, and then switched it off. With no other boats about the dolphin continued to give Beata his undivided attention, frolicking and rolling with her, sometimes hooking her with his penis and towing her along. For three-quarters of an hour Freddie stayed on the surface, or just beneath it, being wound up slowly like a clock spring until it seemed he could contain the energy no longer.

Suddenly he left Beata and came straight for me. There were cheers from the boat as he started to leap backwards and forwards over my head. The film interview with Eileen was abandoned. I could see the cameraman pointing his lens at me, and then the view was obliterated by an immense blow on my face as Freddie, who had hurled himself into the air, fell backwards on top of me, knocking the mask from my face. I disappeared under the water in a flurry of bubbles and stars. I thought the camera that was hanging around my neck would be ripped from its strap. No sooner had I got my face above water than Freddie thumped down on me again in another of his spectacular backward flips. As I surfaced I was thankful I had kept all of my teeth which were still ferociously biting my snorkel tube. Instinctively I felt to make sure I still had my camera. At the same time I became aware of the people on the boat who were jubilant at the performance and quite unaware of the force with which Freddie had struck me. Then, as quickly as it had started, the show was over – or so I thought. I put my facemask back in position and breathed through my snorkel tube.

Freddie had gone back to Beata and was swimming round her excitedly while I clung to the side of the boat for a breather. When I realised that Freddie had not yet burnt up all of his accumulated adrenalin, I became worried about Beata's safety and immediately swam towards her. Just as I approached, Freddie again hurled himself high in the air and fell backwards on top of her, pushing her completely under the water. I was very close by and saw her disappear beneath the surface. I knew she would bob up again because she wore no weights and was incarcerated in a thick Neoprene wetsuit which would act as a lifejacket. Even so, I also knew that it would be a terrifying experience for her. I grabbed hold of her and held on as Freddie reared out of the water and flipped back, pushing us both below the surface. Bill swam towards us and tried to divert Freddie's attention, shaking the egg rattle that had so fascinated the dolphin on the previous day. This diversionary tactic did the trick, and Freddie calmed down until he ceased his aquatic aerobatics altogether.

In the turmoil both Beata's fins had come off and were floating away. I held her, reassuring her that she was safe.

While she pleaded with me to take her back to the boat, I insisted that we should recover the fins and that she should put them on again. Although she was very frightened, she was totally forgiving of Freddie. As time progressed she had lost all fear of being in the water and had transmitted to the dolphin her rapidly increasing confidence. Anyone watching her with Freddie would have been unaware of Beata's incompetence and inexperience in the water.

I realised that a considerable amount of blame for the incident rested with me. When first I had entered the water, I engaged in some very strenuous games with Freddie, wrestling with him and holding on to his fins as we rampaged through the water. Our encounter was as vigorous and uninhibited in terms of physical contacts as those of a rugby match which, rugby fans will know all too well, often result in injury.

It was not until I got back to the boat that the full extent of the damage became apparent. I was sporting a beautiful black eye which was becoming more lurid by the minute. The sight of this souvenir of my encounter with Freddie did nothing to relieve the trepidation with which Eileen, who had quickly climbed back into the boat when the situation became rumbustious, viewed her next encounter with the dolphin. She need not have worried. When she returned to the water, with fresh make-up on and her hair dry and fluffed up, Freddie behaved with perfect decorum. By the time she had finished her piece to camera, with Freddie gently cruising in and out of frame, the rain was starting to come down and boats were leaving the harbour. Relieved and smiling, Eileen knew she had a good finale for her film.

When we returned to the harbour, the water was deep enough for us to go alongside the steps. I loaded my car and set off for home. It had been an exhilarating day, and I knew that I would soon be back with other companions, from Australia and Germany, for yet another television film.

*

While the ancient Volkswagen was drawing to a standstill, Estelle already had the driver's window wound down and was giving me a bright smile.

'G'day, Horace. It's great to see ya, mate.' The unmistakable Australian accent erupted at full volume. 'Wow! Have we had a journey? Sorry we're late. The car broke down in the middle of London. Outside Harrods, would you believe, surrounded by Rollers. It cost 206 quid to get fixed. That's more than the car's worth. What a rip-off.'

Before she was out of the car Estelle had finished a high-speed account of how it had been towed from one of the capital's busiest thoroughfares to a garage in Sloane Square. I knew Estelle so well I could immediately visualise what happened.

'This is Siegfried. You know him,' she said, as her companion and his two girls extricated themselves from the camping gear crammed into every cranny. 'I've got this great idea for a film.'

By the time introductions were over and we reached my front door Estelle had finished a detailed description of what she planned to do in Amble and had moved on to how they would continue the film in Dingle.

Estelle Myers rattled through life like an express steam train that didn't have to stop to take on water. Her energy was boundless. One of my friends once remarked that 'the trouble with Estelle is that the world is too small for her'. Another described her as a 'cosmic hustler'. I thought of her as a 'global catalyst', initiating and speeding up what she saw as the dolphin message to turn dreams into reality.

Estelle's mission to change the world started after a number of encounters with a group of dolphins off Cape Tribulation, near Cairns in Australia, in 1980. She claims that by thought transference or telepathy they gave her three instructions. 'One was to organise a planetary pause for peace once a month – in which people round the world would quietly link their minds in thoughts of peace.' Our aggressive behaviour, she said, was a direct result of the separation that occurred at birth, and in future children

Three Musketeers and Sky's the Limit

should be born from water into water. 'I was to initiate a programme of underwater birthing,' she told a reporter from the *Canberra Times*. The third message was to help free captive dolphins and 'learn from their instruction a way to create a world of harmony and peace.'

When I first met Estelle in 1981, she was already committed to this global mission. Since then, almost single-handed, she had achieved a good many of her aims, selling her home every other year to raise finance. She did everything on trust. Estelle openly admitted that she was able to sustain her daunting, cavalier, globetrotting lifestyle only with the help of a sympathetic bank manager.

She once worked for the newspaper magnate Rupert Murdoch in New York and was a maestro media manipulator. She could organise a press, radio or television interview in whatever country she happened to be – a talent she had put at my disposal several times. She was a compulsive communicator, got very excited about her own ideas, and those of others like me, and wanted to tell the world about them instantly. Estelle was made for the computer age and suffered withdrawal if she was without access to a PC. In the time it takes a civil servant to have a cup of tea she would have computer-processed her latest experiences and ideas and faxed them round the world to her global network of contacts – of which I was but one. Her faxes usually ended with her small logo and a statement in bold capitals:

WE ARE ONE – WON – NOW

BEGIN NOW – WON – ONE

HEAL WITH LOVE

Sometimes Estelle was disappointed that not everyone responded to the love she so generously dispensed. Indeed her powerful personality and open criticism of male dominance – especially in the field of medicine – made her a few enemies, and this upset her. You didn't have to see her to know when she was playing with her grandchildren – you could hear her from several blocks away. In the quiet village where I live on Humberside the arrival of Estelle Myers

71

was like a thunderbolt striking the church. This time the impact was to be short-lived. After spending Saturday introducing the foreign visitors to some of the more quaint aspects of English village life, which included the local wine circle's annual barbecue, I saw them off on a sleepy Sunday morning.

It was grey and pouring with rain by the time Estelle and her party arrived in Amble in the late afternoon. As they searched for somewhere to pitch their tent Siegfried wanted to turn round and quit the dismal place. The smoke and the dreary conditions were too stark a reminder of the industrial heartland of Germany from which he had just escaped. But you couldn't be despondent for long with Estelle to organise everything.

They were all set up by the time I arrived with a film crew from Sky Television. My role was chiefly that of underwater cameraman, while Bill Bowell, who had remained behind after the last location shooting, was to be the support performer for the undisputed star of the film, Freddie the dolphin.

I soon tracked down Bill, talking into a microphone held out to him by the irrepressible Estelle who was conducting an interview for her Australian radio programme. Once everyone and all the gear was safely aboard the *G. Jennifer*, we set off downstream towards the harbour entrance.

Within moments of passing the jetty Freddie was with us. Gordon, our skipper, urged somebody to get into the water quickly or the dolphin would lose interest. Siegfried and Estelle both kitted-up while I waited patiently. Estelle was her usual effusive self, and I was not surprised to see that the dolphin did not give her his undivided attention. When Bill entered the water, she had no chance at all. Freddie stayed with Bill for the next half-hour. This was wonderful from my point of view for it enabled me to get footage of Bill shaking his magic egg rattle with Freddie in shot. I was in full diving kit and could easily sink to the seabed simply by deflating my lifejacket. There, in an attempt to attract Freddie to me, I started digging a hole with my knife – something that had been irresistible to the dolphin in Dingle.

Freddie, on the other hand, ignored me completely and stayed with Bill. I managed a few short sequences of Freddie with Siegfried and his children, but the dolphin wouldn't oblige us by swimming up into the circle formed when everyone linked hands – the shot that Estelle wanted. There could be no doubt who was master of the situation.

By one o'clock we had most of the footage we required, so we broke for lunch, and in the afternoon the film crew interviewed people at different locations along the pier. One of the last to talk to camera was Anita, a girl of 20 who had come to see the dolphin with her boyfriend Graham. She was subject to bouts of severe depression and had even taken an overdose in an attempt to do away with herself. She said she had come from a harsh background, and when she was in hospital her father could not understand why she did not simply pull herself together. What had stopped her attempting to take her life again was her dream of dolphins. She began to paint them and longed to swim with a dolphin. After coming to a public talk I had given she decided to pay a visit to Amble.

Anita described vividly the dire state in which she found herself when she was sucked into the black well of depression. She was quite emphatic that she would rather have both her legs cut off than go through it again. This was something I found hard to comprehend; for me, the thought of having my legs off seemed utterly devastating. In view of my compulsive nomadic behaviour I could think of little worse. When I made this point, and asked Anita outright if that was what she really meant, she resolutely reaffirmed what she had said.

Bill had a long talk with her and assured her that the dolphin magic would work for her, just as it had worked for him. Gordon told her that the best time would be early in the morning, before other activities began in the harbour mouth. As we parted company we all agreed to reassemble at the Lifeboat Station at 7 a.m. the next day.

The sun was shining when I awoke, but a mist hung over the river valley and I was concerned that a sea fog (or sea fret, as it was known locally) might change our plans for the day. At the Lifeboat Station above-water visibility allowed us to see across the river and no more. The harbourmaster did not like Gordon going out in such conditions, for divers in the water posed a hazard at the mouth of the river when visibility was poor. But within half an hour the sun burned through the mist enough for us to set out.

I wondered what Freddie got from his interactions with the various people – myself, or Anita, for instance. Even with one person his behaviour could vary greatly and induce different moods. I could encourage him to jump out of the water, but there was no way in which I could *make* him do so. He always decided what the game was to be and set the rules. Freddie was the master. I acknowledged that.

Today he decided we should just have a gentle swim together. There was none of the rumbustiousness that had characterised our games together a few days earlier. I was reminded just how vigorous those were when I had to be given eye make-up to disguise the bruising.

I learnt later that after her encounters with Freddie Anita was able to cope much better with her bouts of depression and was doing well as a student at art college.

Such was the magnetism of Freddie that there was a distinctly international flavour about Amble that July. When the visitors were not out swimming with the dolphin, they gathered round my parked car like iron filings to a magnet, especially when the boot flap was open. Among those who joined the throng as I packed away my gear was a healer and therapist who wore a dolphin necklace with a crystal attached to it. She told me she was planning to move to Amble, and maintained that the dolphin conversed with her by means of some form of telepathy. In this way Freddie had told her to put away her camera. She said that many people thought her crazy, but she did not find it at all out of the ordinary for she worked with Chakras – an Indian word for points on the body through which energy can enter, the very existence of which was also questioned by some.

Other members of the multi-national Freddie-lovers club were American-born Barbara Jäckli and her daughter Anya, who lived in Switzerland with a Swiss cell biologist, Peter Bioz. They were friends of Estelle's, and Peter had been using her film *Oceania* as the basis of a lecture series. He was very serious, concerned about the future of the planet, and was questioning his way of life. The dolphin intrigued him as a role-model.

To put the dolphin experience into perspective, I suggested we should all go back in time to a period before the British had colonised either Australia or America. So that afternoon we paid a visit to Walkworth Castle, which dated back to the twelfth century. There we roamed the crumbling ruins, with Estelle filming in her usual raucous fashion. It was a perfect day. There was little wind and the sun shone out of a cloudless blue sky.

After lunch we walked along the river and examined the ancient bridge before hiring a boat and rowing upstream to a hermit's cave. It was carved out of the soft sandstone rock, and despite a notice indicating that landing was strictly forbidden, we made our way to the entrance, which was padlocked. It was an extraordinary place. Peering inside, I could see that the ceiling had been carved into the same shape as the vaulted ceiling of a church. Siegfried climbed in through one of the windows. That only served to make the whole adventure more exciting. His two young daughters became quite concerned that they might never see their father again after watching him disappear into the mysterious dark interior.

That evening, back in Amble after clambering round the barrier on the jetty – which also said passage was forbidden – we assembled at 8 p.m. on the end of the south pier for a final celebration. A dozen wetsuited snorkellers were coming back to the stone steps. Never before had I seen Amble in such a holiday mood. Freddie put on a show for us at the mouth of the river, occasionally swimming with the groups of snorkellers who went out to see him and then going for a feed, tossing his catch in the air before consuming it. Bill, who joined the party, reminded us of the time he saw Dorad the Dingle dolphin bring a huge salmon to him and how the water was filled with scales that shone. I produced my didgeridoo and Estelle produced a bottle of Champagne and some trout caviar which she spread on biscuits and distributed to our group. It was a grand finish to her visit to Amble. The sun hung like an orange paper lantern and very slowly moved towards the western horizon where Walkworth Castle, in soft brown silhouette, punctuated the distant skyline which could just be seen through layers of pink-tinted chiffon mist. It might have been a scene from Camelot, in contrast to the impression of Amble imprinted in Siegfried's mind when he had arrived just three days earlier.

I pondered on the meaning of it all. So much of what had happened seemed like a dream. Where did dreaming end and reality begin? Fortunately I had been able to capture many of the extraordinary happenings on film and via television I was again able to sprinkle a little dolphin dust into the lives of many people who otherwise might never have even been aware of its extraordinary power.

· 7 ·

Indecent Behaviour

The ten-minute feature made by Sky Television News centred on Bill Bowell and how dolphins had brought happiness into his world after more than a decade of severe depression. The irrepressible Estelle Myers also appeared in the film, talking exuberantly about the dolphin's penis. In the circumstances, she said, using such a sensitive part of the body as a hook to tow people along must be seen as a gesture of trust on Freddie's part. Exposing it in this way, under voluntary control, for social manipulation was only to be applauded. Her eloquent observations reflected something I had seen and spoken about many times before – even as long ago as in my Yorkshire Television film, *Ride a Wild Dolphin*, in 1976. I assumed by now it was fairly common knowledge, just one aspect of the normal behaviour of solitary male dolphins when they interact with swimmers.

What happened next revealed the danger of making any such assumption about what people understood of dolphins. From an impromptu straw poll I discovered that many of the older generation still thought of dolphins as fish and not air-breathing mammals. To these people, the idea of a dolphin employing its penis as an auxiliary arm was quite absurd. In contrast young people, reared in an age in which condoms were freely discussed, seemed to see nothing odd in a dolphin using its penis for manual dexterity.

For the majority between these two extremes, the subject served only to focus their own prejudices and inhibitions. Most sought escape from further emotional entanglement by turning it into a joke; others, more openly embarrassed, quickly diverted discussion to less contentious issues.

Some wanted to be open-minded. After all, sexual symbols were used everywhere in our consumer society for selling everything from newspapers to underarm deodorants. They tried to rise above their conditioning and were prepared to see the dolphin as an alternative species, uninhibited and not subject to the codes of human society. With a brain as large and complex as ours, at least the dolphins were not obsessed – as were we – with creating and acquiring possessions.

One person I knew who gave a lot of time and energy to considering the feelings and rights of all living things, especially animals, was Alan Cooper. As a professional gardener he was more familiar than most with the forces of nature. He wanted to put right what he saw as the wrongs his fellow humans inflicted upon innocent animals and deplored their use in research experiments and for testing cosmetics. Alan Cooper involved himself in animal welfare projects and lived by his principles. He was well-built, physically strong, a fine example of the fact that consumption of meat is not essential to maintaining a high level of athletic activity. He cycled from Flamingo Land in Yorkshire to Windsor – a distance of 286 miles – in less than a day, on a sponsored ride to raise funds to bring about the abolition of the dolphinariums at the beginning and end of his journey.

I first met Alan in Morecambe in March 1990 after a talk and film show I had given at a rally to free Rocky, a dolphin held there in solitary confinement in a grubby pool a stone's throw from the open sea. After my presentation he told me that he intended to go to Amble to see Freddie. He said he had seen my film about the dolphin Donald and the exposure of his penis.

'What do I do if Freddie does the same thing to me?' he inquired.

'Just treat it as normal behaviour,' I replied. 'He can flick it out and retract it like the blade of a penknife. He may even tow you with it.' With that I turned my attention to one of the other people who were crowding round to speak to me.

Alan Cooper subsequently became a frequent commuter to Amble, taking the train from Manchester to Alnmouth and camping out near Amble. He spent many hours in the water with the dolphin, usually going in to swim with Freddie from the end of the South Pier. Bad weather and cold water were no deterrents: the two of them swam together in all conditions.

Alan got to know Freddie in all his moods and usually adapted his own behaviour to suit that of the dolphin. There were times when they just swam quietly side by side, or rolled over and over one another. At other times, if Freddie was in one of his explosive moods, he would leap back and forth over Alan who did his best to respond. Sometimes Freddie would hook his penis into the crook of Alan's arm, or behind his knee, and tow the delighted man through the water. Occasionally Alan held on to Freddie's dorsal fin and was pulled along. He had read enough to know that the bones in the dolphin's flippers correspond to those of the human hand and that careless handling can cause them to be dislocated, so he was careful not to hold the pectoral fins if he felt the game was becoming too strenuous.

Estelle Myers happened to witness one of their swims when she first arrived in Amble. Later she told me she had never before seen such a tender and loving relationship. Of course Alan preferred to be on his own with Freddie, or with his friend Andrew and others who genuinely had an interest in dolphins. Although he liked people to see Freddie, in the hope it would raise their awareness to the plight of dolphins in captivity, Alan tended to keep clear when tourists were crowding into the sea. He understood full well that such was the bond between himself and Freddie that the dolphin was unlikely to pay much attention to anyone else while he was in the water. So when he saw a boat loaded with passengers in wetsuits approaching Alan would sometimes leave or return to the pier so that others could enjoy Freddie's company.

In keeping with this generous spirit, Alan was prepared to abandon his swim on 28 September 1990 when the G.

Jennifer came chugging down towards the harbour mouth. Upon recognising one of those in the boat, however, he changed his mind. That person was Peter Bloom, the curator of the Flamingo Land dolphinarium, whom he had seen five days earlier when he and a colleague visted Flamingo Land as paying customers. They had sat through two performances and had videoed the pool and parts of the show to illustrate the conditions in which the dolphins were kept. Afterwards they had discussed with the trainer and Peter Bloom – not acrimoniously – the rights and wrongs of keeping dolphins in captivity.

It was clearly a difficult situation for skipper Gordon Easton who wanted to please those who had paid to go out in his boat to see the dolphin. He was aware that Alan Cooper and Peter Bloom took different points of view and that each had produced leaflets on how to behave with Freddie, which they had distributed in Amble.

The Bloom leaflet contained commonsense advice, but also warned that continued physical contact could lead to over-excitement, frustration and even aggression. To some, this appeared to be a thinly disguised publicity stunt to deter the public from swimming with Freddie and direct them instead towards Flamingo Land.

Cooper's leaflet, boldly entitled PLEASE HELP TO KEEP FREDDIE SAFE, was more comprehensive and based upon a similar pamphlet which International Dolphin Watch had produced to help safeguard Simo, the friendly wild dolphin which lived off the coast of Wales. Among his points was the following:

> One aspect of swimming with Freddie is at some stage he may rub against you exposing his penis. Do not be alarmed, this is normal social behaviour amongst dolphins. However, if this makes you nervous or uncomfortable, then consider leaving the water.

In bold lettering, the Cooper leaflet ended with: 'You have seen performing dolphin "clowns" in dolphinariums. These dolphins were like Freddie, living free until they were kid-napped from the sea.'

FREDDIE IS A COMPLETELY WILD
DOLPHIN WHO HAS DECIDED TO
ALLOW HUMAN FRIENDSHIP AND
CONTACT, HE DESERVES OUR
RESPECT AND PROTECTION.

Bloom was fighting a battle to safeguard his livelihood in an industry that was heading for extinction in Britain. The number of static and mobile display tanks had decreased from thirty-six when the first shows based at Flamingo Land went on tour in 1966 to three in 1990. In the winter of 1966 dolphins were made to perform in a tiny circular plastic tank in the old tram sheds in Leeds. During the intervening years our knowledge and understanding of all animals, especially dolphins, has increased immensely. To many people, the removal of individual dolphins from complex social groups in the ocean, and their subsequent imprisonment as circus entertainers in tiny pools, was morally wrong. Some measure of this change in public attitudes can be gauged from the fact that a few weeks after a campaign entitled *Into the Blue*, initiated by Zoo Check, was launched by a major newspaper in 1990 enough money was raised to return Rocky, the dolphin incarcerated at Morecambe, to the open sea.

Many saw Peter Bloom's predicament as not unlike that of a slave trader desperately trying to stave off the collapse of his business enterprise. Among those actively pressing for its demise was Alan Cooper.

It would not be unreasonable to assume that the dolphin-arium curator would be less than pleased to see Alan Cooper. He knew there was a group in the boat who had come to do their own story for a newspaper. If Alan remained in the water the journalist and his photographer were unlikely to get what they wanted. So he told everyone this, saying that the reason why Alan retained Freddie's attention was because he was masturbating the dolphin.

The actual words used, and later given to the police by the reporter in a signed statement, were: 'You won't get near. He is wanking off the dolphin.'

In his statement to the police, made about one month later, Peter Bloom admitted that he did not personally see the act of which he accused Alan Cooper. Nor did anyone else at the time, although two people claimed they saw Alan manipulating the dolphin's penis after Bloom had left the boat.

Three days after the incident was alleged to have taken place the police were notified – a time lapse which provided ample opportunity for all in the boat to communicate with one another and discuss what action to take.

The police questioned the boatman Gordon Easton on 3 October 1990. He told them that he had seen Alan swimming with the dolphin on the day in question. Part of his signed statement read:

> The behaviour of the dolphin with Alan Cooper was no different to the way it behaved with other swimmers or divers in that he can often be seen with an erection even when there are no persons in the water. I could see nothing unusual in the way either the dolphin or Alan Cooper was behaving.
>
> We were in sight of Alan Cooper and the dolphin for most of the time we were out which I estimate as about 2 hours.

Alan Cooper meanwhile was blissfully unaware of what was said in the boat or what happened subsequently. For Alan it was typical of the swims he had had with Freddie many times before. The dolphin had exposed his penis – but that was not at all unusual. He gave the incident little more thought until Wednesday 3 October, just when he was about to return to Manchester, when Gordon told him he had been questioned by the Sunderland police.

It is easy to see how the situation arose. Those in the boat would have been emotionally wound up. They had travelled all the way to Amble for a dolphin encounter, full of eager anticipation. They had set off down river in the company of Peter Bloom, who seemed a personable man and self-proclaimed dolphin expert. Then, just as the dolphin came into view, their hopes were dashed because someone (according to Bloom) was out there masturbating the creature. They did not see what he said was happening. Freddie certainly stayed with the man in question, and sometimes the dolphin's penis was exposed. Why should they disbelieve what they were told? It would have been unnatural if they had not been incensed and outraged.

After Bloom and others had given their statements to the police someone informed the press and most of the daily newspapers in Britain carried the story at the beginning of December. *The Sun* featured it on the front page under the huge headline POLICE PROBE DOLPHIN SEX ATTACK. Several people contacted the police who confirmed the complaint but would not reveal the name of the supposed assailant because the matter was sub-judice. Both Bloom and I were quoted in *The Independent* by Alex Ranton who reported me as saying about the use of Freddie's penis, 'He can use it voluntarily, like a human's arm. It sticks out at an angle and he will deliberately manoeuvre it into the crook of your arm and his penis will pull you along.' Bloom's response to this was, 'That's a load of rubbish. To pretend there is nothing sexual involved is deluding oneself.' Earlier in the same article Bloom was reported as saying: 'There are several people involved: it's an increasing problem with tame dolphins in the wild. In Dingle Bay a few weeks ago I saw a stark naked woman running into the sea shouting, "Come on Funghie, I love you." Dolphins bring out the best and the worst in people.'

When he read the reports in the newspapers Alan was distraught.

On 20 December Alan Cooper was arrested at his home by a policeman who informed him that a complaint had been made to the Northumbria Police about an indecent act with a dolphin in Amble on 28 September. He was taken to Longsight Police Station in Manchester, where he was questioned in the presence of his solicitor, Guy Otten. When he heard that Bloom had told those in the boat that he was 'wanking' the dolphin, Alan protested strongly. 'It's lies, pure lies.'

The cross-examination continued for an hour and a half. Alan became progressively more convinced that, because of his anti-dolphinarium campaigning, Bloom had initiated a 'dirt campaign' against him. The police said it was alleged that Alan had been masturbating the dolphin to make it more aggressive and thereby deter other people from swimming with it.

Alan replied, 'Bullshit!'

He stated emphatically that he had never attempted to masturbate Freddie, nor even thought of doing so. He also made it quite clear that he thought the business in which Bloom was engaged, namely the capture and commercial exploitation of dolphins, was immoral and that the situation in which he now found himself had been contrived by Bloom in retaliation for his efforts to get the Flamingo Land dolphinarium closed down.

At the end of the interrogation a sergeant told Alan that, while he was in his cell, police had searched his house and removed certain documents, including a poem called *Freddie* and two albums of photographs.

Alan told me later that this upset him more than the interrogation, and that is stressful enough in any circumstances. I could understand why he felt this way. I had dedicated my book, *Dance to a Dolphin's Song*, to Peter Worswick, a very sensitive man who took his own life when his collection of dolphin photographs was accidentally ruined. I knew that Alan was paying a high emotional price for the stance he had taken against injustice. He viewed dolphinariums as prisons in which dolphins, innocent of any crimes, were incarcerated for life. It was ironic that if the court found Alan guilty, he could be sent to prison.

A very distressing aspect of the affair for me was that as the Honorary Director of International Dolphin Watch I received mail from some of our members who, after reading the newspaper reports, expressed their disgust for the pervert who was abusing Freddie. They had already decided that Alan Cooper was guilty. In no uncertain terms, they let me know what they would do if they got their hands on the person who could perpetrate such an evil act against a dolphin.

Before the trial Alan's name and address were not mentioned in the press, but with a bit of detective work any person could have found them out. Some did. Alan received death threats, frequent silent and abusive phone calls, and a large amount of unsolicited mail.

On appearing at Alnwick Magistrates Court on 15 May 1991, Alan Cooper was committed for trial. The case was subsequently heard at Newcastle-upon-Tyne Crown Court in December. As an expert witness I sat through the entire proceedings.

I had seen trials innumerable times performed by actors, but it was the first time I had seen a court in action in real life. Apart from my personal interest in the subject, I was fascinated by the ponderous process whereby the court attempted to find out what really happened. It was like panning for gold. A muddy slurry of outright lies, half-truths, dimly remembered facts, clearly recalled events, imagined happenings and sheer fantasy were sieved and sifted in the hope that the nuggets of truth, gold and shiny, would emerge. It took more than four days to isolate and clarify what actually took place during a couple of hours off the coast at Amble over one year earlier.

The process began with a reading of the statement of offence: 'Committing an act outraging public decency.' The so-called particulars of the offence were then read out. They were: 'That Alan Cooper, on 28th day of September 1990, committed an act of a lewd, obscene and disgusting nature and outraged public decency by behaving in an indecent manner with a Bottlenose dolphin to the great disgust and annoyance of divers of Her Majesty's subjects within whose purview such an act was committed.'

The judge addressed the jury of twelve. He explained that, after listening to all the evidence, and having identified what they considered to be the truth, it was then up to them to decide individually if the behaviour of the accused amounted to an act that would outrage public decency.

The case began with Prosecuting Counsel calling in a series of witnesses, including Peter Bloom, each of whom gave their own version of what took place. They were followed by witnesses for the defence, and finally by the defendant himself, although he was not obliged to do so.

The hearing was not without its lighter moments. In opening for the Defence, Anthony Jennings QC told the jury that they should not apply human concepts of sexual behaviour to dolphins. Human beings – apart from at rugby club dinners – did not use their penises to greet each other. Also, humans, unlike dolphins, do not use their penises for domestic purposes, such as pushing the supermarket trolley. Referring to me in his summing up, Jennings commented on the number of books I had written and described me as 'The Ruth Rendell of Dolphins'. I took it as a compliment.

The court burst into laughter when Defence Counsel introduced a video showing Freddie, penis exposed, playing with swimmers. 'This is the closest we can get to calling the dolphin as a witness,' he said. 'He doesn't speak English.' He requested that the video be entered in evidence, together with statements from experts such as Dr Peter Evans, who were called upon to confirm my pronouncement that cetaceans used their penises in a social as well as a sexual context.

Anthony Jennings, who was assisted by Mary McKeone QC, conducted his questioning brilliantly, identifying and highlighting one flaw after another in statements made by the witnesses for the prosecution. Some discrepancies were obvious; such as the colour of Alan's wetsuit. One of those who was most outraged by what she saw, and who identified Cooper as the culprit, said he was wearing a red wetsuit. In reality Alan wore a pale blue wetsuit with yellow arms.

Other discrepancies only came to light as a result of detailed questioning. Two of the witnesses, who claimed that they barely knew Bloom and would not therefore have colluded with him, were revealed to be close acquaintances, one of them even going on holiday with him.

It appeared to me that most of those involved had unwittingly been drawn into a situation from which they could not escape. Having decided on their version of what they thought took place, they were not prepared to deviate from it, despite the contradictory evidence that Defence Counsel presented to them.

Among the witnesses called for the Defence was Doug Cartlidge, an ex-dolphin trainer who had access to the inside world of the dolphinarium industry. He revealed that Peter Bloom had attended a conference where the subject of counteracting those opposed to dolphinariums was discussed. Among the counter-attack recommendations were targeting the leader, getting those involved labelled as 'animal activists', and initiating expensive litigation – which was precisely what had happened in Alan's case.

The gowns, wigs and setting added to the theatrical nature of the event. There were certainly moments of high drama. For instance, no one knew what would happen when Defence Counsel took the gamble of calling two witnesses who had made statements for the Prosecution. They were a husband and wife who had gone out on the *G. Jennifer* in order to swim with Freddie. The wife's signed statement to the police (28 October 1990) concluded: 'Mr Bloom, the dolphin expert, explained to the people on the boat the act that was taking place. I was totally disgusted at the actions of the man when I was informed that he was masturbating the dolphin.' The husband's statement was similar.

The gamble paid off.

Under cross-examination they both agreed that they were indeed totally disgusted by what they were *told* was happening. Yes, they did see Alan, and they could clearly see that the dolphin's penis was exposed for some of the time, but neither of them saw Alan committing the act of which he was accused, despite the fact that they had ample opportunity to do so.

On the fifth day the barristers put their respective cases

before the judge finally summarised all that had happened. The atmosphere was tense when the four men and eight women of the jury retired to come to their decision. Was Alan Cooper guilty or not guilty?

The jury was out for about an hour, which is an unusually short time for such hearings. When they returned, their spokesman told the silent court in a very powerful and clear voice that the verdict of the jury was unanimous.

They found the accused 'NOT GUILTY'.

A roar of cheering went up in the public gallery. Outside Alan was besieged by reporters. He was filmed and photographed surrounded by supporters who bore banners and placards proclaiming the verdict a victory in the fight for the freedom of dolphins in captivity.

Doug Cartlidge made a statement to the press in which he said the case exposed a sinister plot by the dolphinarium industry to intimidate and discredit a man of sensitivity and integrity who was campaigning against keeping dolphins in prison.

I made the point that a great deal of public money (£37,500 according to one later estimate) had been spent on a lesson in dolphin behaviour. I also raised the subject of the validity of observations on captive dolphins, upon which some of Bloom's statements were based. I proposed that all future research should be carried out with the voluntary co-operation of free dolphins in the open sea.

For his part, Alan thought he was completely vindicated, and he would continue his mission to see that the captive dolphins at Flamingo Land and at Windsor were returned to their natural home in the open sea.

What did not come out in the trial was that Alan had taken his mother to see Freddie before he was accused. His mother was deeply distressed at what happened and died shortly before the trial. Her death added to the deep anguish Alan felt at being accused of what he regarded as an abusive act and a betrayal of trust. Knowing his innocence, he was sad that his mother never saw the day when her son was exonerated.

Most reporters agreed that the case should never have gone to court. None the less it was a small milestone in British legal history. Cynics said it would have been even more sensational if Alan had been found guilty.

Friday 13 December 1991 was a good day for Alan. It ended a year of heartache and uncertainty. He celebrated his victory the best way he knew. He went to Amble for a swim with Freddie.

· 8 ·

Whose Circus Is It?

A few weeks after the trial of Alan Cooper I was visited by Virginia McKenna, who made her name as an actress with such feature films as *Born Free* and *Carve Her Name With Pride* and who is now a dedicated conservationist. She and her husband Bill Travers led the campaign to set up Zoo Check eight years previously to monitor the welfare of animals in captivity. Their small team investigated the dolphinarium industry and launched a successful appeal through the *Mail on Sunday* newspaper to rescue Rocky and, after a suitable period of rehabilitation, return him to the open sea. A few months later two more dolphins, Missie and Silver, who were held captive in a small pool of chlorinated water in Brighton, where they never saw daylight, followed the same escape route.

Now Virginia was writing a book, appropriately called *Into the Blue*, not just about the release programme, but also covering many aspects of the lives of dolphins. This included their relationship with humans, hence her visit to me. On the same day as her visit (7 January 1992) a newspaper cutting arrived in the post with the headline 'Set the Dolphins Free'. Beneath it was a picture of Alan Cooper with a dolphin-shaped coffin and a group of supporters outside Flamingo Land. He was urging the public to boycott the park until the three dolphins currently held there were set free. The newspaper reported that Mr Cooper had recently been cleared of sexually assaulting Freddie and included a quote from him stating that the court case had highlighted the plight of dolphins in captivity. A spokesman for Flamingo Land said the park was involved in dolphin *research* and their dolphins were not unhappy. The clear implication of this statement was that such a worthwhile role outweighed any misguided notion about the morality of keeping dolphins imprisoned in a concrete pool.

As soon as I read the word 'research' I thought of Tricia Kirkman's explosive outburst when she had heard that scientists carrying out research were putting used tampons into the sea in an effort to prove (scientifically) that another friendly dolphin, Simo, was more readily attracted to females in the water. We were at a social gathering and one of the scientists concerned was in the room when she heard what had been going on.

'How dare they do it!' she roared.

Hurriedly I dragged her outside for fear that she would assault the man. It was a spontaneous display of anger on her part. She did not have to ponder the question: in her black and white world the issue was clear. Such an abuse of Simo's friendliness was utterly unforgivable.

I tried to reason with her. After all I was a scientist. I put forward the usual arguments about advancing the frontiers of knowledge, helping to save human lives, and the rest. Tricia calmed down a little until I tried to justify dolphin research using parallel arguments. This was not the right thing to do. She immediately hurtled into headlong attack on me.

'What a load of rubbish,' she exploded. 'What benefit do the *dolphins* get out of it?' Before I could respond she detonated her final word on the subject, 'NONE!'

The vehemence of her attack made me reconsider my position on the ethics of using any animals in research.

The cutting about Alan Cooper was on my desk when Virginia came into my study. I told her of Tricia's attitude to research, and that despite my background in pharmaceutical research in which large numbers of animals were used in laboratory experiments, I had been through a profound heart-searching on the question. Now I felt I could say honestly that, if I were to start again, I would not engage in

some of the animal studies I had conducted in earlier years –
even if my career depended on it.

Virginia taxed me further by saying 'Dolphinarium
owners are guilty of exploiting dolphins, we all know that,
but aren't you equally guilty of exploiting dolphins by taking
people out to swim with them?'

She drew attention to Dingle, where people banged on the
sides of their boats to attract the dolphin and chased after
him if he moved away. As a result several dedicated conservationists had expressed the view that such interaction
should be limited, or perhaps prohibited altogether, on the
basis that it was reasonable to watch but not to interfere
with the 'natural' behaviour of such friendly dolphins in the
wild.

I said I thought that in places like New Quay in Wales,
and the Moray Firth in Scotland, the semi-resident pods of
dolphins should be allowed to continue to do what they did
without being harassed. Sometimes they put on spectacular
shows, jumping for the sheer joy of it. Such spontaneous
displays brought great pleasure to those who happened to be
around at the time. In such situations I felt we could watch
without undue interference.

The situation in Amble, and in Dingle, where there were
solitary dolphins which had sought out human company,
was different. We deliberately lured the Dingle dolphin who
then followed the boat, to a cave where we filmed him.
And, yes, there were occasions when he had disappeared
and after a while we had sent out the inflatable to see if we
could entice him back. But we had never harassed him. He
always came of his own free will. By the summer of 1991,
however, whenever it was calm the bay was packed with
pleasure craft laden with paying customers. Funghie-
watching had become big business. When all the associated
revenue was taken into account, the total income reached a
staggering figure, millions of pounds, according to some
estimates. Funghie had become Ireland's number one
tourist attraction.

If some people held that making money in such a way was

immoral, then they were entitled to that view, and I would not argue against it. Neither would I argue against the assertion that Dingle harbour had become a circus. It was a circus. But who was the ringmaster? The people all thought that they had Funghie under their control. Surely the opposite was true? The dolphin had the humans under his control. He whizzed from one boat to another, encouraging those on board to perform their outlandish tricks for his amusement. There were the hull thumpers, the engine revvers and the shouters who called out to him, but they weren't as entertaining as those who waggled brooms or boathooks in the water for the dolphin to inspect and poke with his beak. One of the tricks he most liked his artists to perform was to throw an inflated ring in the water and pull somebody along with it.

He deduced that humans were quite intelligent. They learnt quickly. But he always kept them on their toes – it didn't do for any of them to think that they had cracked it. He never let them perform the same routine twice. Sometimes he could get an entire boatload working well – their full repertoire in fact; hull thumping, engine revving, vocalising, boathook splashing and even a towing. When that happened, it was his signal for other boats to motor towards him, as invariably they did. Then, just as they started to home in, he would disappear and tweak a little cabin cruiser that was going straight out to sea without taking any notice of him. The cheek of it! Some of these humans take a bit of disciplining. If they ignored his first signal he would give the whip crack – a big jump just in front of the bow. They always responded to that command.

A group of humans he found very easy to train were the canoeists. On quite simple commands he could get them paddling like hell, racing after him. They were also quite good at paddle splashing, and he even managed to get some to dribble water on to his beak as he popped up under the paddles when their canoes were stationary. It took a bit longer to get them to roll their canoes, and some of them never managed it. But if they did, he gave them encouragement by wagging his head when they were hanging upside down. The poor things couldn't stay in this position for very long.

The most difficult he found to train – and in some ways the most rewarding – were the divers, especially those with cameras. He got them to perform all manner of tricks. Stone bashing was the most common. They all learnt that very quickly. The technique he found to work best was to swim briefly in circles round a boat (to get the occupants excited) while they were getting kitted-up, and then to go away and do something else the moment they entered the water. He didn't bother with them again until they had really mastered the trick, or the *behaviour*, as he preferred to call it. What they had to do was to swim down to the bottom, find a couple of stones and knock them together. The point was that, no matter how far away he was, he knew where they were when they had succeeded with this trick because he could hear the sound wherever he was in the bay.

Even so, he often let them work at the trick for some time before going over to see how they were getting on. He noticed that some of them seemed to get quite annoyed if he didn't come quickly. Sometimes they even shattered the stones. If they progressed as far as this, he felt they were doing well, and might even go on to air cylinder banging – usually with their diving knives – which, with the cylinders on their backs, required a degree of gymnastics and therefore could be regarded as more advanced training. By comparison, teaching them the anchor chain rattle behaviour was relatively easy.

The zenith of the underwater performance, however, was mastered by only a handful (or finful, as he preferred to call it) of the hundreds of divers he trained up. They were the ones who learnt to build sandcastles on the seabed, usually by excavating the sand with their diving knives. These gold medal trick performers from the human world had to be given a very special signal – apparent rapt attention, with head nods. Funghie never understood why it was that those who managed this remarkable achievement seldom told fellow divers what they had done. Perhaps it was modesty, or shyness. When asked in the boat afterwards how they managed to get the dolphin's attention for so long, they never admitted to building underwater sandcastles.

Although I treated the subject in a lighthearted manner, I was quite seriously saying that we had to be careful not to be zealously over-protective of Freddie or Funghie. Alan's court case had shown that some people are inclined to assume the worst. Any person photographed chucking an empty beer can overboard with the dolphin in frame could well end up with his picture in the paper and be accused of throwing the can *at* the dolphin. A huge outcry could ensue, fuelled by the vast majority who felt protective towards all animals. The outcome of my hypothetical story could well be that people like me, and others with legitimate reasons, would be allowed to swim with wild dolphins while the general public would be excluded. I am totally opposed to the formation of what would amount to exclusive clubs of scientists and policemen.

So I stick to the view that we should not attempt to deprive Freddie or Funghie of human company. My argument is that these are dolphins which, of their own free will, deliberately choose to consort with humans. It is their choice, not ours. They would not do it if they got nothing out of it.

Rocky, who was captured as a youngster, should have been imprinted by humans. Yet, when he was set free in 1990, after eighteen years in captivity, he immediately ceased to associate closely with them. The same applied to other dolphins I knew had been released. Despite enforced contact with humans, upon which they had been totally dependent for food, none of them sought human company once they were free.

If Freddie and Funghie were disenchanted with human company they could simply swim away. They could be gone in a minute and, if they wished, never follow a boat or swim with a human again. The choice was theirs, and they chose to stay. My reading of their situation was that the more time people spent in the water, the more the dolphins enjoyed it.

'What about those reports of Freddie becoming aggressive?' Virginia asked me.

'I don't think you should blame a dolphin if he bites somebody. They rake one another with their teeth when they are together in groups. I have seen dozens of dolphins in remote places with rows of parallel white scratches made by teeth. They are rumbustious animals that play rough among themselves and sometimes with humans. One dolphin I knew bit through my wetsuit and drew blood when he wanted to play with the aquaplane I was holding on to. Freddie has given me a black eye. Dolphins sometimes play rugby with humans. If you play those rough games you must expect to get the odd injury. I see that as a matter of education – not for the dolphins, but for humans. That's why International Dolphin Watch distributes leaflets advising swimmers how to behave in the water with Freddie. If the game gets too vigorous, then swimmers should attempt to stay still. The dolphin will soon get the message. We also appoint ambassadors who, at key places, will take people out to see the dolphins and advise them how to behave in the water.'

'But what about Monkey Mia in Western Australia,' said Virginia, assuming my monologue had finished at last. 'They feed the dolphins there. Surely that's undesirable and should be stopped?'

I was familiar with the situation at Monkey Mia, which I had described in my book *The Magic of Dolphins*. I told her that one of my favourite pictures in the book was of me standing alone in the sea with a little Aborigine girl and two dolphins at my feet.

'If you look carefully at the picture,' I said, 'you can see a rainbow and it comes right down to little Rebecca's head. The picture was taken in 1986 by Rebecca's father, who was paddling into the sea with my camera.'

I launched into another monologue during which I informed her that the caravan/camping site which was there then had now been swept away and replaced by a hotel.

8 At Monkey-Mia in Western Australia (*above*) dolphins have been coming to the beach to mix with the holidaymakers for more than twenty years

9 Recently a school of friendly dolphins (*below*) has been coming close inshore to play with divers at Rockingham Bay, south of Perth

10 After the court case Alan Cooper went to Amble to swim with the dolphin Freddie (*above*)

11 The Dingle dolphin (*below*) was friendly but did not encourage people to touch him, although that was what most tried to do

Monkey Mia is in a remote wilderness region known as Shark Bay about 800 km (500 miles) north of Perth in Western Australia, and there are now three generations of dolphins which come to the beach to swim between the people who wade into the sea. There are well over a hundred dolphins in the bay; many have been given names and can be identified by their dorsal fins. The dolphins visit the beach frequently, but not regularly. Fish are available on site to feed them and clearly they enjoy the handouts. Dolphins have been coming to Monkey Mia for more than twenty years. It was once the only place in the world where you could be fairly sure of an encounter with a free, friendly dolphin, or even a group of dolphins, at the water's edge.

When I was there I respected the wishes of the proprietors of the camp site, Wilf and Haze Mason, not to go swimming with the dolphins, but just stay in shallow water. In that way, they had argued, everyone got a chance to make contact. Grannies with their grandchildren, and people of all ages in between, paddled at the edge of the sea to talk to, and perhaps touch, Holey Fin and her daughter Holly and several other dolphins who cruised along the shoreline close to the sandy beach.

Over the years the number of people visiting Monkey Mia has increased steadily. The route from Denham – a dirt road when I drove there – has been surfaced and now half a dozen wardens patrol the beach to manage the crowds that arrive by the busload.

'Surely that's exploiting the dolphins, isn't it, Horace?'

I could not agree. Once again, it is entirely the dolphin's choice to come in and take fish. They would still choose to associate closely with humans, though probably less frequently, if they were not fed. I also pointed out that the fish they are given is only part of their diet. They spend long periods mixing with other dolphins far out in the bay where food is abundant.

'But the purists say that dolphins should not be fed,' Virginia said, continuing to play devil's advocate.

'Well, that may be their view, but I don't agree with it,'

I persisted. 'I have heard that the dolphins at Monkey Mia sometimes bring in fish from the bay and throw them to people on the beach. What should we do in these circumstances? Throw them back? Purists can be killjoys.'

I really don't see the situation at Monkey Mia as being fundamentally different from feeding birds. Should we get rid of all our bird tables? After all, birds in the wild don't eat bread. Tits don't eat peanuts in normal circumstances. Having them come close does bring a great deal of joy to millions of people.

'Nature goes for integration not isolation,' I said. 'Anyway, I've got some good news for you. Yesterday a video arrived from Estelle Myers. It has some sequences taken a few weeks ago at Monkey Mia, but it also shows other places nearer to Perth.'

We left my study to watch a fascinating ten-minute film. It included Bunbury where, in 1989, the local council financed a successful attempt to recreate a dolphin encounter situation similar to that at Monkey Mia. Visitors are able to call in at an information centre manned by volunteers before going down to the water's edge to feed and gaze at the dolphins when they come into the beach from Koombana Bay.

Useful spin-offs arose from this enterprising scheme. The presence of friendly dolphins has increased the awareness of the local townsfolk of the need to prevent and control pollution. The water in the bay is now monitored more frequently, and consequently those responsible for the disposal of waste are much more careful about what they discharge into the sea. Steve Honor, who manages the site, lists ten other benefits to the community in his report for the management of the Bunbury Dolphin Trust.

The highlight of Estelle's film was entitled *Dolphins – Future Visions*. At the small seaside suburb of Perth, called Rockingham, she introduced a young man by the name of Terry Howson who had given up his job as an aircraft pilot to become a boat skipper. 'A pilot,' he said in the film, 'is just a glorified bus driver.' He has since befriended about a hundred dolphins in the open sea. Those he doesn't know by name he knows by number. We watched enthralled as he took Estelle to meet his friends – the dolphins. They were clearly delighted to have him zooming among them while clinging to a little electric underwater scooter.

'Wow!' said Estelle to the camera with her usual gusto. 'What a way to go dolphin dancing.'

Neither Virginia nor I could disagree with that! Terry did not feed the dolphins. Man and dolphin played together in a joyful harmonious game in which there were no winners, and therefore no losers.

Was this really a glimpse of the future? It was certainly the way both of us liked to think it would unfold.

I had something even more futuristic than that on my desk. It was a fax copy of a letter sent to me by Estelle on the same day – 6 January 1992 – that it was submitted to the Lord Mayor and City Councillors of Rockingham, Western Australia.

The Honorable Lord Mayor, Ladies and Gentlemen,

Following the last meeting on the 12th of December 1991 at 5.00pm, Council Chambers, Rockingham.

We now wish to submit our design ideas to develop with your co-operation a program which could see the building of a unique environmentally friendly floating structure to house a research, education and re-creation centre in Mangles Bay, Rockingham.

You will find in the next few pages an introduction to the concept of Aquatecture (art & science of building on and below the Ocean) with a schematic design proposal for the floating structure.

Yours faithfully,
Joseph Keszi.

It was accompanied by an artist's impression of a floating platform incorporating an underwater observatory attended by dolphins and a diver. It was based on the principle of a huge free-floating fishing float, weighted at the bottom with ballast. The architect, Joseph Keszi from ORCA (Oceano-graphic Research Centre for Aquatecture), who had won an international competition in Japan for his revolutionary design, also enclosed a cartoon which appeared in the *New Yorker* magazine in 1955. It showed the evolution of man, out of the sea, and then back into it again.

Current evolution theory has it that the dolphins, once land animals, evolved into marine mammals. So I will venture to suggest that if the cartoonist, Ed Fisher, is right, and we do eventually return to the sea, we shall be following the dolphins. Thus the dolphins have already made the evolutionary journey that we are now embarked upon.

Now there's an interesting thought, which raises even more questions – such as, how long it will be before we catch up? If ever.

· 9 ·

Opening the Mind

After graduating in chemistry at London University I spent many years of my life working in scientific fields that included human and veterinary medicine and often involved the use of radioactive isotopes. Early in those days I developed a passion for diving. As founder of The Oxford Underwater Research Group I was keen to explore the limits to which humans could safely extend their activities underwater. People were diving deeper, for longer, with and without breathing apparatus. How much further could we go?

Off the coast of the Isle of Man in 1974 I found the answer was looking me in the face. Nature, it seemed, had already done what I was seeking to do. The dolphin didn't get the bends, it didn't suffer from narcosis, it could resist the cold, it could swim at incredible speeds, it had no fear of sharks, and it could even 'see' underwater in zero visibility by means of self-generated sound. The dolphin was a miracle of evolution – the ultimate aquatic mammal.

So the dolphin I met in the Irish Sea at that time (which I called Donald) became the model for my studies of the science of diving. By understanding the differences between his physiology and mine there was a possibility that I could extend my ability to explore the oceans – not as a man locked inside a pressure-resistant capsule, but as a free-swimming diver.

Gradually that idea was displaced when I became aware of Donald's curiosity. I knew that many of the creatures I had encountered under the sea were curious. I could lure an eel, a blennie, or a lobster out of its hole by arousing its curiosity. One false move and it was back in again like a spring-loaded bolt. Donald was different. He was quite un-afraid, and would watch me so intently that I gained the distinct impression he was actually studying me.

I remembered reading a book by the American research scientist, Dr John Lilly, which among other things discussed the relationship between Margaret Howe and a dolphin named Peter who lived together in an experimental facility on St Thomas in the United States Virgin Islands. For two and a half months they were together for twenty-four hours a day, Margaret sleeping in a bed just above the surface of the shallow pool which was their joint quarters. Lilly was trying to prove the error of the view, widely held by scientists, that only *Homo sapiens* was capable of speech, language, thought, imagination and emotions. Even if the data he provided was inconclusive, he certainly opened a channel in my mind. Could Donald become more than just a delightful and curious companion?

In the open sea I would not have the control that Lilly enjoyed in his experiments, which were conducted in as near as possible laboratory conditions. But if Lilly was right, and intelligent, two-way communication and learning processes took place between humans and dolphins, then I had an advantage which could take my studies leaps and bounds ahead of his. Communication between two individuals involves the active participation of both. In Lilly's experi-ments the dolphins were captive. Any intelligent input by the dolphins was severely limited by their dependence and inferior status. They had no option but to join in, and devel-oped strong bonds with those who fed them. Lilly himself initiated and controlled what happened.

Human-dolphin roles would be reversed at sea. Being independent and free, the dolphins could, if they wished, initiate their own attempts at communication, to which the humans could respond if they were sensitive and intelligent enough to do so. At the same time, of course, humans were free to attempt their own experiments, but if the dolphins felt so inclined, they could simply swim away.

This new approach was dependent upon one vital ingredient – the active co-operation of one or more dolphins. Although dolphins associate with humans, often swimming in the bow waves of boats, such contacts are usually transient. It would appear that humans provide only temporary diversions from the usual social activities the dolphins enjoy with their own nomadic family groups.

When I met Donald I realised that I was in a rare situation. Here was a dolphin who definitely wanted to associate with humans and perhaps even communicate with them. I did not want to do anything that might cause him to deviate from this attitude, so I determined that no matter how much I wanted his co-operation I would never attempt to confine him in any way. I would have to go wherever Donald chose to roam. And roam he certainly did. From the Isle of Man he crossed to Dun Laoghaire and then journeyed to South Wales and Cornwall. Knowing that dolphins can 'see' with sonar, I decided to investigate how the dolphin perceived his own image reflected in a mirror. My experiments might have petered out when Donald vanished in 1978. But I was able to resume them with the arrival of Jean Louis off Brittany and Percy off the Cornish coast in 1982. When these two dolphins disappeared, Dorad (alias Funghie) and then Freddie arrived on the scene.

Meanwhile public interest in wildlife, and especially in dolphins, had developed rapidly. Encouraged by this, I put more time and energy into International Dolphin Watch which had grown rapidly. As its Honorary Director I was receiving a host of mail from all over the world.

Operation Sunflower, and the astonishing public response to my television film *The Dolphin's Touch*, brought hundreds of letters from people who were suffering from depression, some long and pitiful. I myself was coming under stress. My time and emotions were beginning to be stretched to the limit.

I wanted to help those in real need but it was impossible to take them all out to see Freddie or Funghie. There was the 'audio pill' – dolphin sounds set to music – to capture artificially the experience of meeting a dolphin. But I had to do more to simulate an encounter with a wild dolphin in the sea.

An idea came to me after my first swims with Freddie in June 1989. If I wanted to simulate the experience for others, then it had to be done in water – in a dolphin therapy pool. Like most solutions, it seemed obvious once I had thought of it. The user would float, or swim gently, almost completely submerged in a pool of isotonic saline at body temperature. Dolphin images would be projected into the water. Music and dolphin sounds would be transmitted through the water by means of underwater loudspeakers, so that those immersed would perceive the sound through their entire bodies in a manner similar to that in which dolphins receive sound information from their surroundings in the sea. With the water in the pool similar in physical characteristics to the overall body fluids, the swimmers would be virtually part of a continuum. In other words they would become one with dolphin sounds and energy.

How it would be built, where it would be built, when it would be built and who would finance it were all questions I delegated to the gods. I knew it would happen sometime, somewhere, somehow because of the 'snowman principle'. This was something I had evolved for my personal use. It fitted the new circumstances in which I found myself when I ceased full-time employment in the pharmaceutical industry. Once free from the compulsive, competitive need to make profits for shareholders, I could afford the luxury of abandoning the main tenet of most management systems which are based on the 'make it happen' principle. I discovered what I am sure many people know, that before anything can happen a basic idea has to be formulated clearly. It then needs to be dispersed, rather as silver iodide crystals are to make rain. In the 'snowman principle' thought seeds incorporating the basic objective are sprinkled without restraint (and that is important) into the ether. Speaking metaphorically, crystals of ice form on the seeds and float down as snowflakes. What is remarkable is that they always form a snowman. It may not be quite the snowman envisaged in the first concept, but it is all the same a snowman. Applying the principle in practical terms involves coming up with a proposal, spreading it around without fear that somebody else will steal the idea, and then letting it happen. The secret is to encourage – never to push.

Some of my associates, especially those in business, were amazed at my supposed innocence. A few even called it 'airy-fairy'.

Naive and airy-fairy it may be – but it works! On the basis that you don't discard something that succeeds, I applied it to creating a dolphin therapy pool.

Nuclear power is based upon a controlled atomic explosion. Sub-critical masses of enriched uranium are put together until they reach what is called a critical mass. At that stage, if the chain reaction is not brought under instant control, the released energy is so great that the whole system is blown apart. My metaphorical dolphin mass became critical in March 1990. It happened at an 'Alternatives' meeting in St James' Church, Piccadilly, in the heart of London, where speakers were invited from time to time to express their views and theories on a wide variety of so-called New Age subjects. Among them, Rupert Sheldrake had been able to talk freely about his concept of morphogenicity, which links all life into a common memory and energy field through a dimension of what he called natural consciousness. Such creative and spiritual alternatives to accepted Western thought were not necessarily the views of the Church itself, and when I accepted the invitation to speak I did not know what to expect. I was given very little information and didn't seek to satisfy my curiosity because I was so busy. Besides, I enjoy not knowing what lies ahead.

It was dusk when I arrived and found the large cavernous building lit with candles and filled almost to capacity. There were elements of a religious service in the way the evening was conducted. There was meditation and a couple of hymn-like songs were sung. In between these I spoke, with the aid of a microphone which was essential, about the mysterious healing power of the dolphin. I showed a film, dipped into such subjects as a global dolphin consciousness and the Australian Aborigine Dreamtime, liberally sprinkled thought seeds about creating a pool in which to simulate an encounter with a dolphin, and left.

What had taken place in the ethereal atmosphere felt vague and unreal. I could barely remember what I had said. Two weeks later I received a letter from Evelyn Mason, someone I did not know who said she was the Development Officer of Scunthorpe MIND, inviting me to open a new Mental Health Community Centre in the heart of the town.

I had a limited knowledge of the old steel town of Scunthorpe apart from flying over it in the Yorkshire Television helicopter from which I looked down through a pall of smoke on a grey, barren landscape of lifeless buildings, dull as lead and soulless. It was the kind of place I liked to pretend didn't exist.

I had heard of the MIND organisation but knew little of how it operated. I soon discovered that it was outside the National Health Service and was supported by statutory grants and voluntary contributions.

The Scunthorpe Centre was autonomous but linked to a national organisation based at 22 Harley Street in London. Their policy was to dispel the ignorance, discrimination and neglect that for too long had shaped attitudes to people who suffered mental illness and distress. Its Charter urged that, whenever possible, such people should not be shut away but should be treated as individuals, and every effort made to restore them as full and valid members of the community. Despite the fact that only 10 per cent of mentally distressed people were treated in mental hospitals, 90 per cent of all mental health funds in Britain were swallowed up by these crumbling institutions. MIND's objective was to fill the gap by providing local centres with a welcoming social environment in the form of a café, a library and recreational facilities in which a confidential counselling service could be brought to the mentally ill while they remained in the community. In Scunthorpe the new MIND Centre was a bright and airy sanctuary with a warm and cosy atmosphere where people could discuss and share their problems. The modest red-brick building, once a printing works, was open to anyone suffering from mental and nervous stress, regardless of their financial resources.

Scunthorpe itself was in the throes of depression of a different kind. A century ago it consisted of three tiny villages. With the basic ingredients for the manufacture of iron in the neighbourhood – coal, limestone or chalk, and iron ore – it was the obvious place to set up a steel works. Newly industrialised Britain had an enormous appetite for the metal. Mining and steel manufacture were labour intensive and huge numbers of workers were attracted to the area. Scunthorpe boomed. The villages were engulfed, farms disappeared into sprawling housing estates.

During the Second World War the town provided one of the most vital raw materials for the manufacture of arms, and the flourishing postwar period lasted into the late Sixties when virtually everything that was made could be sold. But by then Japan and the Third World countries were starting to use their huge human resources to produce labour-intensive goods more cheaply, and the British heavy manufacturing industries went into sharp decline. Thousands of jobs were shed in Scunthorpe. The loss of earnings affected not only those directly involved, but a multitude of others dependent upon the basic generators of wealth – steel and coal. Despondency crept like a damp fog through all levels of society as thousands lost their jobs. How could they, as individuals, as simple honest workers, bring about the vast changes necessary for their survival? The people of Scunthorpe felt helpless and inadequate: some could no longer afford the payments on goods they had bought on credit; others couldn't pay the rent, and those at the very bottom of the newly created human scrapheap with no fixed address could not claim welfare benefits.

One of the defence mechanisms nature provides for those

who feel no longer able to cope with the pressures that society imposes is simply to cut off emotional contact with fellow humans. We sink into a black quagmire in which our minds are numbed and from which we consciously tell ourselves there is no escape, despite knowing subconsciously that this is not true. Evelyn Mason told me that more than 60 per cent of those who suffer from mental illness remit naturally; in other words, they get better of their own accord. The role of the new Centre was to provide a path out of the mental quagmire.

I wondered if the healing power of dolphins could help the people who used it. I could provide *Dolphin Dreamtime* audio-tapes for those attending the Centre and their therapeutic benefits could be enhanced by watching *The Dolphin's Touch*, a video recording of the film about the uplifting effect of the Dingle dolphin. But I could do more. I told Evelyn about the dolphin therapy pool. She was immediately receptive to the idea. But where could such a dolphin pool be located? Evelyn had a brainwave.

The Church of St John the Evangelist close by was a huge Gothic building isolated amid a mass of modern structures. To my mind, it was by far the most impressive building in the town, yet it was empty and boarded up. It was one of those places that the developers would have loved to demolish if it were not protected as a listed building. There it stood in a sea of concrete – a magnificent, proudly defiant monument of brick and stone.

I had found a possible location for the world's first dolphin therapy pool, or more accurately, the location had found me.

Days later I arrived at the Seekers Trust at Addington Park, near Maidstone in Kent. I was taking part in a one-day conference on the theme 'Healing Planet Earth' and shared the platform with Baroness Edmee di Pauli and Sir George Trevelyan, who had written a number of books in which he incorporated many of the old Christian values into a new type of spiritual awareness. I had never heard of the Seekers Trust until I was invited to contribute to the meeting and discovered it to be a non-denominational centre for prayer and spiritual healing set in 37 acres of woodlands and gardens. These included a peaceful, rose-filled Garden of Remembrance. According to the literature, the Seekers were founded in 1925 by an outstanding healer who was guided by Dr Lascelles, a medical practitioner already in the spirit world, whose specially devised prayers proved to have powerful therapeutic effects in their own right or in conjunction with medical treatment. At the end of the presentations, which were given in a chapel, the audience showed their appreciation by holding their arms aloft and oscillating their hands – a Tibetan style of silent applause that I found very moving.

It was a strange stepping-stone in my journey to the land of arguably the most spiritual people on earth whose history, if accounts are correct, goes back some 40,000 years. I was on my way to Australia to participate in the Second International Whale and Dolphin Conference at Nambucca Heads, about 300 miles north of Sydney. The meeting would be attended by a group of Aborigines and their Elders, upon whose sacred land the event was taking place.

I had several reasons for wanting to make contact with Australian Aborigines whose culture kept them in a stable balance with the land and waters that sustained them. It was unique because of their complete geographical isolation. At school we were told that the Aboriginal way of life was a remnant of the Stone Age. But it seemed to me that a long-lived culture which was so harmonious with the environment might have something to teach modern societies in which consumerism and growth were bringing about an imbalance that was threatening man's future on the planet.

The presence of Australian Aborigines at an International Conference on Whales and Dolphins was just one of the imaginative ingredients that the organiser, Australian Kamala Hope-Campbell, introduced into the programme. It was she who, in 1983, founded BRETH, a breathing and meditation technique which she claimed enabled humans to perceive the messages that whales and dolphins were transmitting, and which she used to guide her own actions. She bought a site, Hyland Park at Nambucca Heads, on which to create the International Cetacean Education and Research Centre, where interdisciplinary research on whales and dolphins could take place. She approached Bill Smith, a traditional custodian of the Komilaroi Tribe, to bless the land. In doing so she gave the centre a strong spiritual link with the indigenous people. As a step in the fulfilment of that dream she organised the First International Whale and Dolphin Conference in 1988 and it brought together some of the world's leading conservationists, natural scientists and academic authorities on cetaceans.

· 10 ·

Aboriginal Men of High Degree

The Aboriginal Group, most of whom had English-sounding names, were camped a short distance away from the cabin occupied by my wife, Wendy, and myself throughout the conference. They were interested in the didgeridoo I had acquired on my previous visit, and I received my first proper lesson in playing it from Ray Kelly junior.

The didgeridoo is the traditional musical instrument of the Aborigines. It is made from a tree trunk that has been hollowed out by termites. A suitable length is cut off and any debris left inside is pushed out. It is then scraped until it is smooth. The outside is commonly painted with a design, called a Dreaming, which portrays an aspect of Aborigine life, usually what Westerners would call a mythical story. Mine had a water Dreaming and depicted a journey from a riverbed to the surface. It had a stylised picture of a bottom-dwelling crayfish and a barramundi fish for mid-water. A water-lily at the end of the pipe indicated arrival at the surface.

A smooth ridge of soft beeswax on the rim at the end of the pipe provides a seal round the lips, which should be pursed and pressed into the tube. Gently blowing through the lips causes air inside the tube to resonate and the note is varied by altering the shape of the buccal cavity and the tension of the lips. Getting some noise out of a didgeridoo is not too difficult, but learning to circular-breathe is another matter. This is a technique which enables the player to produce a continuous drone. It takes a lot of practice to discover the knack of breathing in through the nose while blowing out through the lips, using the cheeks to expel the air trapped in the mouth.

The drone of the didgeridoo is deeply spiritual. It has its counterpart in cultures more recent than that of the Australian Aboriginals. In his book, *Pi in the Sky – A Revelation of the Ancient Wisdom Tradition*, Michael Poynder refers to Ogham – 'a secret language that somehow reflects the energy of the creative force we call God.' He states that Ogham (pronounced OHM) is 'the same sound as the OM or AUM universally known in Eastern religions . . . It is a representative of the cosmic sound of the universe that pervades everything.'

Every didgeridoo is different and produces different sounds when played by different people. The player becomes part of the sound system, the air in the windpipe and the lungs altering the resonance of the air in the wooden pipe.

Ray Kelly told me that to play the instrument properly the performer needs to formulate in his mind the image or feeling he wants to convey and then concentrate mentally on projecting it while blowing down the tube. A listener in a receptive state can then interpret the player's message.

A good deal of native Aboriginal music is concerned with animals that play an important part in the everyday life of those who live in the bush. The musical image can be made more realistic by mimicking animal sounds and overlaying them on the drone. The bark of a dog is one of the easiest to produce and recognise. A series of 'boying' 'boying' 'boying' sounds can depict a kangaroo hopping with giant bounces through the scrub.

The corroboree is a ceremonial dance around a fire which, like most events in Aboriginal life, happens when it happens. Such disregard for precise timing can be very frustrating for those brought up in the Western world where most people's lives are dominated by preplanned timetables – going to school or to work, even going on holiday. Ray suggested that I should take my didgeridoo to the corroboree which the Conference organisers hoped would occur some time during our stay.

The spirits smiled on the conference and the corroboree did in fact take place. The ground vibrated to the stamping feet of the Aborigines and the sound of the didgeridoo mixed with the crackle of the fire. It was a celebration, and was probably also one of the first occasions on which the organiser of a conference attended by delegates from many parts of the world openly acknowledged that it was taking place on ground that was sacred to the Aborigines. Kamala Hope-Campbell told those attending she felt privileged that the gathering had the consent of Bill Smith, and an Elder, Uncle Lenny De Silva, who was highly respected in Aboriginal society. That consent was not mandatory, and the conference could have taken place without it, but for Kamala, who was striving for a more tolerant, egalitarian and peaceful way of life in which the whales and dolphins were her guides, it was important that the customs and rights of the Aborigines should be acknowledged.

The invaders who arrived in Australia in 1788 and quickly overwhelmed the Aborigines regarded themselves as superior in every way. Their policy was to suppress the culture of the Aborigines and integrate and assimilate them into the religions and lifestyle of Europe. They wanted to sweep away the indigenous population and their customs, keeping just a labour force to develop and convert what the colonists saw as a virgin land and its resources into a roomier, richer, more pleasant version of Great Britain. Aborigines were prohibited from speaking their own languages, and were forbidden to practice their tribal ceremonies. It was government policy to break up and disperse the tribal and family units. At worst the Aborigines were seen as a nuisance to be exterminated (and indeed that is precisely what happened in Tasmania) or at best as the unfortunate victims of the progress of the whole of mankind into a more enlightened world. There really was no justification for the continuation of the lifestyle of a black population which behaved like primitive savages, ruled by spirits thought to be still present long after the people themselves were dead.

As the Aborigines themselves had no written languages, and did not manufacture anything more permanent than the simplest of weapons and utensils from biodegradable raw materials, all trace of their existence should have disappeared in a few generations. Indeed that is what almost happened. Among the European emigrants, however, there were a few who realised that the indigenous people of Australia should not be dismissed so summarily. One of these was Professor A.P. Elkin, Head of The Department of Anthropology at the University of Sydney from 1933 to his death in 1979.

Professor Elkin studied and attempted to understand the Australian Aborigines, especially the medicine men. His book, *Aboriginal Men of High Degree*, must have been a revelation in its day, for when it first appeared in 1945 Aborigines were included with the fauna and flora in the National Parks and Wildlife Department. Not until the referendum of 1967 in New South Wales were Aborigines recognised as people with rights in their own land.

In a Preface to the second edition of *Aboriginal Men of High Degree*, published in 1977, Jeremy Beckett sought to put the author and his work into perspective:

Elkin's subject is the medicine man. But this term, with its connotations of chicanery and gullibility, scarcely conveys the importance such figures hold for Aborigines. The 'clever man', as some English speakers call him, acquired wonderful powers through direct contact with the beings of the Dreamtime: the rainbow serpent; the sky gods; the spirits of the dead. He has come to this state through a long and rigorous apprenticeship and an initiation of terrors and ordeals beyond those that ordinary men undergo. He is what Elkin calls a man of high degree and his experiences have changed him utterly. He has died and come alive again; his entrails have been taken out and replaced; he has been swallowed by the rainbow serpent and regurgitated; magic crystals have been put in his body; he has acquired an animal familiar that dwells within him. As a result of such experiences, the medicine man can fly and travel over the ground at great speed; he can anticipate events and knows what is happening in faraway places. He can cure and kill mysteriously. He can make rain. He can ascend to the sky world on a magic cord that emanates from his testicles. He can roll in the fire without hurt; appear and disappear at will.

Elkin will not allow the medicine men to be dismissed as frauds and humbugs; nor will he have them reduced to something else. He has been as unsympathetic to explanations in terms of the subconscious mind as he now is to the search for unconscious structures. He finds the notion that shamans are psychologically unstable equally inapplicable to Australia. Medicine men are part of the mainstream of Aboriginal society and culture, despite their absorption in the esoteric . . .

When *Aboriginal Men of High Degree* first appeared there was little likelihood that Aborigines would read it. The few who had been educated to do so had also learned to be ashamed of their heritage. Today the situation is different, and I hope that this book, free as it is of technicalities and jargon, may enable some to re-establish the link.

In the years that elapsed between these words being written and my visits to Australia efforts were indeed made by Aborigines to re-establish their own links with the past. One man did more than most in this direction.

Burnam Burnam was born under the family gum tree at Mosquito Point in 1936. Under the government policies of the day, he was separated from his family when he was three months old and taken to a mission near Nowra before being moved to Kinchela Boys Home. His sister was sent to Cootamundra Aboriginal Girls Home, more than a thousand miles away. Burnam Burnam was educated at the University of Tasmania and played rugby union. At the time he was known as Harry Penrith, but in an attempt to get closer to his Aboriginality he changed his name in 1976 in honour of his grandfather of the Wurundjeri. In the same year he was awarded a Churchill Fellowship.

He toured the continent, trying to get a glimpse of the Dreamtime through the oral traditions of a hugely diverse people who for two thousand generations had managed and maintained a continent. He tried to find out how they lived, what food they ate and the traditions they upheld. The story he uncovered had an inevitable edge of sadness and pain. In 1902 for instance, it was argued in the fledgling Australian Parliament that in the light of archaeological interpretations of the day there was absolutely no evidence to suggest that the Australian Aborigines were humans.

In most areas the invaders who came in 1788 were greeted warmly by the Aborigines who had no idea they intended to stay. The thought of somebody arriving from the edge of the ocean to take away their land was inconceivable to them when every feature in it, and every plant and animal on it, was intimately connected with the Dreamtime, into which their own spirits were intricately woven.

In 1988 a weighty tome, *Burnam Burnam's Aboriginal Australia*, was brought out by the Australian publisher Angus & Robertson in an arrangement with Dolphin Publications. After commenting on the permanence of European architecture, the author wrote in the Foreword:

> In Australia, the land itself is the cathedral and worship is not confined to any four walls. Each step is a prayer and every form in the landscape and everything that moves in it – were put there specifically for the people to use and manage. And the mythical beings made clear the responsibility of the people in preserving and nurturing the environment . . .
>
> I hope the reader will find no bitterness in the story: the past cannot be turned back. The story of dispossession is a sad and moving one, but many of the Dreamtime stories are equally tragic. The challenge of the future is the important issue, and an acceptance of the past is the first step to

a positive future. Australia is now a mix of many nations and the land itself is the ultimate power. No one people have a sole franchise on the ability to feel an affinity with this timeless landscape.

When eventually I met Burnam Burnam in Brisbane, I found him to be a great showman with a wonderful sense of the ridiculous. He had a gold Mercedes and a young white blonde wife. He was a paradox. On 26 January 1988 he had clambered along the beach beneath the White Cliffs of Dover and claimed the whole of England as an act of revenge for the British seizure of Australia 200 years before.

His declaration began: 'I, Burnam Burnam, a nobleman of ancient Australia, do hereby take possession of England on behalf of the Aboriginal peoples. In claiming this colonial outpost, we wish no harm to you natives, but assure you we are here to bring you good manners, refinement and an opportunity to make a "koompatoo" – a fresh start.'

He was seen as a pariah by many of his own people, and by Aborigine rights purists. They despised his self-publicity stunts and regarded him as far too Europeanised to represent their ideals. The ostracism hurt him, but it was counter-balanced by the veneration he received from those who saw him as the creator of a vital bridge between the past and the present.

Most of us now accept that there are brilliant minds in every ethnic group and that those so endowed often attain positions of respect, and sometimes power, in their respective societies. Leonardo da Vinci was born of humble origins in 1452 and became one of the greatest artists and scientists the world has known. The drawings of his inventions, such as the helicopter, were based on an intuitive understanding of the laws of physics which governed the mechanical world in which he grew up. The equivalent Aborigine genius, who had no possessions and lived in close contact with nature, would instead have used his exceptional intellect to explore the spiritual forces that ruled his own existence and influenced everything and everyone around him.

In his book *The Songlines*, Bruce Chatwin puts across the relevance of possessions to the Aboriginals in a cleverly scripted dialogue between the storyteller and Father Flynn – the first ordained Aboriginal to take charge of a mission. He sets up the scene by asking a question about trading and then explains that a shell might travel from the coast to the interior along a route connecting waterholes where men of different tribes would gather.

'For what you call corroborees?'

'*You* call them corroborees,' he (Flynn) said. 'We don't.'

'All right,' I nodded. 'Are you saying that a trade route always runs along a Songline?'

'The trade route is the Songline,' said Flynn. 'Because songs, not things, are the principal medium of exchange. Trading in "things" is the secondary consequence of trading in song.'

In the terse narrative that follows Chatwin reveals how the Aboriginals assimilated their culture in oral traditions expressed as song.

Before the whites came, he went on, no-one in Australia was landless, since everyone inherited, as his or her own private property, a stretch of the Ancestor's song and the stretch of country over which the song passed. A man's verses were his title deeds to territory. He could lend them to others. He could borrow other verses in return. The one thing he couldn't do was sell or get rid of them.

Just as my understanding of the Aboriginals had been partially influenced and shaped by Chatwin's, his were by Karl Strehlow. Chatwin had great sympathy for the author of works such as *Songs of Central Australia*, which he described as 'great and lonely books'. If an author creates a window through which to view a scene, then the quintessence of that scene can be further concentrated if it is processed through a mind as selective, analytical and sensitive as that of Bruce Chatwin.

Strehlow once compared the study of Aboriginal myths to entering a 'labyrinth of countless corridors and passages', all of which were mysteriously connected in ways of baffling complexity. Reading the Songs, I got the impression of a man who had entered this secret world by the back door; who had the vision of a mental construction more marvellous and intricate than anything on earth, a construction to make Man's material achievements seem like so much dross – yet which somehow evaded description.

What makes Aboriginal song so hard to appreciate is the endless accumulation of detail. Yet even a superficial reader can get a glimpse of a moral universe – as moral as the New Testament – in which the structures of kinship reach out to all living men, to all his fellow creatures, and to the rivers, the rocks and the trees.

An important feature of Aboriginal culture is that the knowledge of their lore, which is held by what Elkin described as 'men of high degree', can only be passed on to those worthy of receiving it.

Adhering strictly to this code makes it impossible for most Aborigines and all non-Aborigines to infiltrate the core of their spiritual culture. At first sight this is anathema in a Western world where all information is theoretically available to those with the initiative to search it out and the intelligence to understand it. But it may be a necessary safeguard, evolved over generations, that will help the Aborigines through the critical years that are now upon them. For the record shows that we in the West have a habit of taking what we want, and throwing the rest away. So at this stage it may be wise for them to withhold their knowledge of the power of the spirits and not to release it until we have shown that we are of sufficiently high degree – or, as we would say, wise enough – to handle it.

For a culture to survive for 40,000 years it must be alive. All living things change with the passage of time and are influenced by their environment. So even the Elders, who are openly opposed to change, know that their culture will have to incorporate aspects of the new spirits to which they are now being exposed.

The Aboriginal corroboree is an event which can go on for days, during which people come together to participate in ceremonies and exchange knowledge and views in a social atmosphere with chanting and dancing. That same description could well be applied to the conference organised by Kamala. In the evenings there was much noisy dancing to rock music which, I am sure, would have appeared to an interplanetary time-space traveller as 'primitive' as any footstamping, dust-raising dances performed by the Aborigines before 1788. The conference and the social functions were attended throughout by Aborigines of both sexes who, collectively, wished to share their peoples' dolphin connections with the other participants.

All females were asked to leave the room when the most senior Elder said he was prepared to address the conference on what he described as 'Men's Business'. This, not surprisingly, caused a low murmur of dissent among some of the women present who, if they were not active feminists, were emancipated and independent. However, in deference to the customs of the Aborigines, they left the main hall and had an all-female gathering with the Aboriginal women. From what I was told afterwards it was a totally open, spontaneous, informal and very enjoyable event. They discussed topics in a manner which they would not have done had there been any men present.

Once all the women had left, Bill Smith asked Ray Kelly senior, the father of my didgeridoo tutor, to give the dolphin Dreaming of the area to his all-male audience. He delivered his words, slowly and with dignity. He spoke about the relationship coastal Aborigines had with whales and dolphins, and the respect in which they were held, along with all other animals. He answered a few questions, decided he had said enough, and quietly left the stage with the slightly hesitant gait of someone of advancing years.

On formal occasions in the British Parliament, in the Courts, or in the Church, those of high rank can be distinguished easily by their ceremonial robes. There were no symbols of authority to denote, or to support, the high regard in which the senior Elder who addressed us was held by his fellow Aborigines. An ill-informed observer might have been forgiven for classifying the elderly man, dressed in well-worn western clothes, as a down-at-heel unskilled casual worker – which might well have been the case. A person of his age would have had very little opportunity to do anything else when he was young. He depended solely on his own innate ability and wisdom, first to win the esteem and respect of his kinsmen, and then to project the authority they vested in him.

The meetings of the Whale and Dolphin Conference were conducted in a large hall. It rained so hard during Wally Franklin's presentation that it sounded as if he were receiving constant applause. He told an enraptured audience of the work he and his wife Trish, an historian, had undertaken to bring about a re-enactment of the first fleet of ships which sailed from Europe to Australia in 1788 to set up a new colony. All in all, it took ten years of planning and preparation to assemble a fleet of square-rigged ships and sail them to Australia to celebrate its bi-centenary. During that time the Oceania Project had gradually taken shape in the minds of the Franklins. By 1990 they had a clear objective – after the bi-centennial festivities they would use old sailing ships to raise awareness across the world of whales and dolphins in the open oceans.

Wally saw the effect of first contact between Europeans and the Aborigines as similar to the impact of humans on whales and dolphins. He wanted the re-enactment to redress the situation: those arriving on the sailing ships in 1988 would come in joy and peace, and furthermore they would recognise the rights of the Aborigines.

The Franklins lived in Byron Bay. Wendy and I followed them home and stayed in their house when the conference was over. This pleased me greatly because between them the Franklins had a considerable knowledge of the Aborigines, a great respect for their culture, and they shared with me their understanding of the complex multi-layered philosophy that made up the Dreamtime. They both saw mastery of the didgeridoo as the key to my initiation.

Wally arranged for me to meet and play with the two best didgeridoo players in the district. One was an American, Jim Harvey, who had been taught by Aborigines in the Northern Territory, where the didgeridoo originated. At one time Jim had lived with the North American Indians, whose relationship with the earth and belief in the spirits which lived in all things was very similar to that of the Australian Aborigines.

The other person who helped me considerably in mastery of my wooden tube was a young white Australian mother, Kavi. Wally drove me to her house. She could remember the exact time when she learnt to circular-breathe. It happened one night when she was watching the moon. She said she felt as if a spirit moved into her and she played non-stop for a long time. We sat on her veranda in the damp gathering dusk where she played the most haunting sounds I have ever heard issue from a didgeridoo.

Armed with this new knowledge I carried my didgeridoo to the sacred sites that Wally was eager for me to visit. I found Wally a delightful companion. We climbed together to the top of Mount Wollumbin, which rose to a height of 1,157 metres. It stood majestically in a bowl-shaped valley surrounded by other mountains. Geologically it was the plug of a massive volcano which had erupted twenty million years ago and was responsible for many of the geographical features of the north-east corner of New South Wales. When Captain Cook first saw it, he called it Mount Warning – a warning to seafarers of the dangerous reefs in the area.

The great navigator was unaware of the significance the mountain had for the tribespeople of the area. It was customary for the senior clan leader to be called Wollumbin, which is said to mean 'warrior' or 'fighting chief' of the mountain. Legend has it that the spirits of the mountains were warriors. The wounds they received in battle were the scars on the mountainside. The thunder and lightning were the results of their battles. This is consistent with the origin of the name Wollumbin, which some people say means 'cloud-catcher' or 'weather-maker'. As the derivation of the name implies, the weather can change quickly and dramatically on Mount Wollumbin. But Wally and I were blessed with a day that remained fine for our ascent. In traditional Aboriginal life only fully initiated men could go to the top of the mountain. Now it stands in a National Park and there are no such restrictions on those who wish to climb the trail to its summit.

The foot of the mountain was wooded with giant trees whose size alone inspired awe. Mentally I paid my respects as we climbed. We stroked the trees with our hands, trying to sense what wisdom, message, or feelings they might impart to us. Every now and again I would play my didgeridoo, and I noticed that its resonance changed perceptibly in the close presence of different trees. Did they understand how much I loved them?

As we climbed Wally explained to me how the lore of the Dreamtime was handed down by the storytellers. Half-consciously he took on the same role himself, not just presenting the facts in words, but also managing to impart their spiritual significance by virtue of his own sensitivity. He said that although the life of Aborigines was precarious it was also very stable. They lived in the Dreamtime, and the emotional impact of understanding that was enormous. A man's personal Dreaming merged with the totality of the Dreamtime. Everything in his life was directly connected with Dreamtime. Countless features of the landscape had a Dreamtime explanation which gave them significance. They all fitted into a grand Dreamtime scheme. The exploits of the Dreamtime heroes and villains influenced the shape of the rocks, the colours of the earth, the windings of a watercourse. Such features were tangible memorials of his tribe's creative ancestors. As they themselves were also part of the Dreamtime everything they saw, did, felt and experienced was to some degree sacred.

An Aborigine is not called upon to believe in an unseen god. There is proof positive of the almighty spirit around him. All life is one, and he is part of it.

Most Aborigines stayed within their own tribal territory which was clearly defined. Those who wandered further afield – and those included the storytellers and the wise men – never passed over a tribal boundary without performing negotiations in accordance with ancient laws. They were bound immutably within a grand design which changed little over thousands of years, until that fateful day when the first Europeans arrived.

Therein lay the connection between the cetaceans and the Aborigines. Had the whales and dolphins also been part of a grand stable design, which lasted in their case for millions of years, before sailing vessels and then powered ships brought men, chemically powered weapons, mammon and technology to bear irrevocably on their lives? In two short centuries the whale and the Aborigines had both been pushed to the lip of extinction. But what had become of their spirits? Were they adrift in the Dreamtime, waiting for new physical forms to inhabit?

· II ·

A Grand Design

I was in a state of considerable optimism when I returned to England to plunge immediately into a whirlwind of lecture engagements. These included a residential weekend at the Wrekin Trust in Malvern, which was founded by Sir George Trevelyan as an educational trust 'dedicated to exploring the spirituality of man and the universe'. Among many eminent thinkers who previously had addressed Trust meetings were Dr Lyall Watson, author of *Supernature*, and Professor David Bohm, a physicist considered by many to be Einstein's natural successor. His book, *Wholeness and the Implicate Order*, argued that everything in the universe, animate and inanimate, is directly connected to everything else in one vast unified energy field.

Once again I found myself caught in a spiral of controversy. The other main speaker was Colin Andrews, the author of *Circular Evidence*, who since 1981 had been intently studying the mysterious depressions in fields that had come to be known as corn circles. Some people attributed them to the activities of extra-terrestrials, linking the formation of crop circles with UFO sightings. Others proposed that they were the result of freak weather effects which produced bolts of energy. The hoaxers literally had a field day.

I enjoyed the debates, but they were energy-demanding. I was still recovering from my trip to the antipodes and emotional pressures from other quarters were draining my mental and physical reserves. Close to exhaustion after the weekend, I climbed to the highest peak in the Malvern Hills and played my didgeridoo. Sometimes I sat in silence, just feeling part of the earth and the sky. Sir Edward Elgar, whose home was nearby, found the hills inspiring. I recalled my first visit to this spot on a cycle tour when I was sixteen. Other precious moments from previous visits floated through my mind. Slowly, very slowly, the inner anguish dissolved into a quiet peace.

I realised that, while playing my didgeridoo, I had found a way of communing with nature. It was something I could do privately and I preferred that no one should see or hear me doing it. Somehow it brought me into harmony with the unseen forces. Still I had not conquered the circular breathing that enabled the most skilful performers to play continuously, but persistence paid off. A few weeks later I managed it.

When the moment of mastery came, it seemed like learning to ride a bicycle, but a hundred times more difficult and rewarding. Breathing in through the nose while breathing out through the mouth brought the whole body – and the mind – into equilibrium.

It happened after another Alternatives meeting at St James' Church in London's Piccadilly. This time Kutira Decostard, who played the didgeridoo, was the main presenter. She was supported by a guitarist with a lilting voice, and a West Indian drummer. Several other didgeridoo players of different nationalities wandered in off the streets of London. One of them I knew to be taking time off from busking. I joined in when, quite spontaneously, the moment arose for a group to play together. One didgeridoo player was Australian; Sophia came from California, and Kutira, who was born in Switzerland, lived mostly in Hawaii where she spent many hours swimming with dolphins. It was this dolphin connection that had led me back to St James. For Kutira and Sophia were members of a group of wandering troubadours who spent their lives connecting with dolphins. These latter-day gypsies were far from impoverished; they were perfectly capable of earning a crust, even a gourmet meal, almost anywhere by performing live or selling cassettes of their music.

Kutira was one of a troupe which had earlier stopped off

at my house in Humberside on their way from London to see Freddie in Amble. A short time later I met her and Sophia in Dingle, where we played our didgeridoos to Funghie. The dolphin gave our recitals no more attention than his usual short-term interest in anything new that aroused his curiosity. At the time he was getting into canoes, as they say. The rascally dolphin much preferred rearing out of the water to poke his snout at paddle blades held aloft and dripping with water. Such activities always got the onlookers cheering with approval and the dolphin, a spontaneous showman, invariably responded to the crowd.

There was something pure and honest about Sophia that shone through her voice. The notes she sang in St James' Church were still gliding through my mind like seagulls on an updraught when I boarded the mail train at King's Cross to take me back to Doncaster. Travelling through the dark night, knowing that most other people were fast asleep in bed gave me a strange feeling of isolation that I do not usually feel when I am on my own in the daytime. I sat in an empty carriage, picked up my didgeridoo and started to play as quietly and gently as I could to suit my mood. As I did so, suddenly I found the co-ordination necessary to circular-breathe. After that I played my didgeridoo almost non-stop for the rest of the journey. I was floating high above the planet. The loneliness of the black night disappeared.

Dawn is my most creative time. The moment I wake up I am usually alert and, if inspiration is going to come, then that is the time when it usually does so. Sometimes ideas come tumbling into my mind one after another. If a solution to a troublesome problem suddenly becomes apparent, then at that sublime moment I experience a feeling of euphoria which I feel I should release in an explosive outburst by yelling – 'Yippee!' or 'Eureka!'. But I never do. Instead, silently yet triumphantly, I punch the air with my fist, the inhibited yell remaining like an inflated balloon inside my chest.

That was how I felt shortly after I awoke on the morning

of 8 August 1990. It was after an exceptionally delightful time with Freddie, and I would like to think that maybe he played some part in planting the idea in my mind – who knows? Anyway, it was the moment for a grand scheme, bigger than anything I had thought of before, to manifest itself inside my head. In this vision I saw the dolphin therapy pool as part of a complete and much larger picture within an architectural framework, which in Scunthorpe happened to be the derelict Church of St John the Evangelist. Furthermore, I saw Scunthorpe as a model for other centres, each individually different, but based upon the same broad principle. An important aspect of the scheme was that it should not be a 'take all' situation; we had to give back to the dolphins something in return. If the idea came to fruition, it would be my contribution towards a more caring society which catered for individual human needs and was concerned for the welfare and survival of all species – but especially the dolphins.

Delighted as I was, an idea locked away in my head was of no value to anyone except myself. I knew that I had to make the concept more widely available in the form of a written proposal. Before that, however, I needed to review the situation in order to satisfy myself that I was running on the right lines. Only if I were sure that my project was sound could I hope to persuade others to take it seriously.

I took myself back to the start. We already had MIND, up and running and doing a marvellous job. We also had dolphin therapy, gradually establishing its credibility. We had a dolphin therapy pool, yet to prove its worth. And finally, we had my new idea, which was to join all these concepts together and to add a few more. An important ingredient was to help people develop their natural artistic talents and then use any revenue generated to help dolphins. I wanted to create a wheel of energy in which dolphins help people help dolphins help people.

That was the essence of the plan. So what were the problems and how could the plan be implemented?

The plight of the dolphins was tragic. Millions had been

12   JoJo loved to play
     with Dean Bernal

13, 14 JoJo pauses for a moment (*above*) after hurtling round
like a Dervish when Tim took off with the Manta board

killed accidentally by the fishing industry. Their environment was being poisoned by pollution. Their food was being removed from the sea in ever-increasing quantities. Thousands were still being hunted and killed for sport and for food.

The human problems were also immense, but different. With an estimated one person in ten in the West needing some form of psychiatric treatment during his or her lifetime, there were about six million people in Britain alone who needed help. The most common symptom I noticed among the increasing number of those suffering from mental ailments with whom I came into contact was a feeling of inadequacy, which presented itself as a frustrating inability to cope with simple everyday activities. In a society geared to achievement these people often felt they were social outcasts. By adopting this attitude, they made the situation worse for themselves. What was needed was a mellow sanctuary where people could discuss their problems in a pleasant social environment that did not flaunt the symbols of success or impose financial restraints, where the spiritual energy conveyed by the dolphin would foster hope, joy and love.

It would be called a Dolphin Therapy Centre (DTC), and would incorporate the facilities for giving people support and encouragement to develop whatever artistic potential they had. How many potential van Goghs are there on the streets of towns and cities throughout the world, unable to explore whatever talents they have through lack of help, resources and encouragement? I did not see DTC facilities restricted to painting but encompassing all forms of creative endeavour: writing, painting, sculpture, dancing, music, drama and crafts.

My research suggested that dolphin therapy was less likely to be effective in isolation than when combined with other forms of treatment. These could be either conventional chemotherapeutic medicines, or other complimentary therapies such as reflexology, aromatherapy and hypnotherapy. The DTC would become a friendly meeting place, with a cafeteria, recreation room, library and a television and music room, in addition to quiet spaces for counselling.

The primary function of the centres would be to help people overcome distress, especially damage to their self-esteem. Treatment would be based on installing in those suffering from mental or emotional difficulties the idea that they *can* and will recover. The dolphins and all of the other treatments would be there to enable them to get better themselves. For this, it was important they should be able to mix with other members of the public, and so I proposed to incorporate small retail outlets, such as a secondhand bookshop, a bistro, a picture framing shop and outlets for any art and craft products created in the DTC.

An attractive dolphin therapy pool would be the focal point of a DTC. Money raised from the artistic accomplishments of those who benefited would be used to help dolphins. Thus each Dolphin Therapy Centre would foster the concept of a truly caring society; a society which cared for and responded to the needs of animals as well as their fellow humans; a society which gave something back to dolphins instead of taking from and exploiting them.

Anne Page spoke to me about my ideas on dolphin therapy for a feature she ran in the *Guardian* newspaper in February 1992. After quoting a favourable response to the *Dolphin Dreamtime* tape from educationists and psychologists who had tried it in prison, yoga classes, psychiatric hospitals and in art psychotherapy sessions, she reported me as saying: 'You can measure the healing of a broken arm but you can't measure the healing of a broken mind except by personal comment.' I cited Bill Bowell, who said he was cured by swimming with a dolphin. 'My scientific background could not allow me to accept it. The MIND people said I shouldn't be telling him he isn't better if he thinks he is.'

We must not be surprised if the idea of dolphin therapy seems at all far-fetched to those who have not experienced it. 'We didn't invent radio waves or television waves,' I reminded Anne Page. 'We found out how to manipulate them. Dolphins have been working in the sonic world for twenty million years. I wouldn't be surprised if they've acquired an ability to manipulate waves which at present we don't experience. Until Geiger came along with his counter we didn't know radiation existed, but it was always there and we were always affected by it. However we haven't found a way of measuring dolphin energy.'

We may not know yet how to measure whatever it is that dolphins radiate, but the evidence for its existence is becoming insurmountable.

· 12 ·

How Does It Work?

As the concept of dolphin therapy spread and gained acceptance, an inevitable question was raised repeatedly: 'How
does dolphin therapy work?'

By the end of 1991 it was obvious there was no one simple
explanation. I wondered if the hundreds of responses I had
received by then to the *Dolphin Dreamtime* audio-tape
would give me some leads.

The audio-tape was based on ancient Aborigine concepts.
It took the listener, through music and sound effects, on a
gentle mental journey into a new state of mind – that of a
dolphin. The journey began in a cave. After descending some
steps into another cave full of crystals the listener was
carried by music and words down more steps into a third
cave, full of beautiful plants and birds, before emerging into
a sea filled with whale and dolphin sounds blended with
music. Here the listener joined the dolphins, became a
dolphin, and experienced the joy of drifting freely through
sun-filled waters.

I first met the originator of the tape, Taranath Andre, in
Australia in 1988 and described my response to it in *Dance to
a Dolphin's Song*. Being a hard-headed sceptic, I wondered if
the illusory journey I enjoyed when listening to the tape
while floating in a swimming pool was due to an overdose of
Aussie hospitality. I decided to test it at a playshop at the
College of Psychic Studies in London. To my surprise, every
person in the crowded room, except for those who went to
sleep almost instantly, had some pleasant form of out-of-
body experience. I realised then that somehow Taranath

Andre, who was a healer, and the musician Glenda Lum, had managed to capture the essence of the dolphins. I knew from my background in pharmaceutical research that they had, metaphorically speaking, 'bottled' dolphins. I called the *Dolphin Dreamtime* tapes 'audio pills' and dispensed them through International Dolphin Watch. We sold them to people who could afford to buy them and gave them away to those who could not.

I did not want to become embroiled in clinical trials to prove that my dolphin pills were efficacious. Double-blind cross-over trials with a placebo were a thing of the past for me. Even so, I was curious to find out what effects the tapes had on the people to whom they were distributed in a completely random manner. Listeners were invited to complete the questionnaire enclosed with each tape. Those subject to bouts of depression were asked what effect, if any, *Dolphin Dreamtime* had on their moods. I wanted to find out if the familiarisation process, which is an essential part of the development of our ability to enjoy music, was also necessary before the mood-changing effect of *Dolphin Dreamtime* could be fully appreciated. So I asked if the experience changed for them after hearing *Dolphin Dreamtime* more than once. Finally I invited general comments. There was no compulsion to complete the form but I did assure those who returned the assessments that the information would be treated in confidence.

As it turned out, my inability to let go completely of my past training in medical research brought many bonuses. The first of these was the astonishing diversity of people who benefited from my audio pills. One woman described in great detail exactly how it cured the pain in her back. This brought me unadulterated pleasure, for one of the pharmaceutical companies I had worked for spent millions of pounds on their research for a 'low back pain' remedy. To be fair, we did discover a number of substances with profound analgesic activity, but none that worked specifically in the lumbar region. The company stood to make a fortune if we had been successful.

The young head of the Pharmacology Department at that time (he is now a Professor at an Australian university) was particularly outspoken in his views on those who controlled his budget, and I wondered how he would have reacted upon learning that serendipity, in the form of a dolphin, had found our Holy Grail. Neither I, nor he, if he looked at the completed assessment form, would suggest for one moment that I had stumbled upon a universal cure for low back pain. I had no doubt this was a case of stress-induced pain, and listening to the tape had removed the stress. However, in this instance, the audio pill did have the inestimable benefit of treating the cause, not the symptom, which is still the case for the majority of medicines.

When I launched the concept of the audio pill I was in the fortunate position of having whatever direction I took entirely under my own control. I was dependent upon nobody for a budget and was totally self-motivated. I had made the conscious decision to work exclusively on intuition – if it felt right I did it; if it didn't feel right then I didn't do it. It was as simple as that. I knew I was going out on a limb. If the bough broke I had only myself to blame.

This did not mean that I was unwilling to debate what I was doing. On the contrary, I welcomed constructive criticism from anyone who had an interest in the area I was pioneering. Analytical discussions compelled me to justify a course of action to myself, and change direction if necessary. They also stimulated new ideas.

It was therefore with some pleasure that I received an open and friendly letter expressing interest in my work from Dr John Teasdale of the Applied Psychology Unit of the Medical Research Council at Cambridge.

It contrasted starkly with one I received earlier from an American researcher whose terse introduction led straight into a list of eight questions about dolphin therapy which started with: (1) How do you find dolphins to co-operate? (2) How do you locate dolphins for 'appointments?' and (3) How do you communicate with dolphins? – all quite valid questions if he had the mistaken impression that I sat beside the sea, and that calling up co-operative dolphins was no more difficult than hailing a taxi. The remainder of his questions were devoted to patient selection and included: (5) Are there any factors you can identify in the process of curing the depression (which I had never claimed) other than the instillation of a broader perspective of life?

I visited Dr Teasdale and, after a stimulating debate on psychotherapy, was introduced to Charlotte Lloyd, then working for her PhD. Charlotte had a special interest in dolphins and offered to undertake the statistical analysis of the Dolphin Dreamtime assessments. I was delighted. I therefore sent her all 57 of the completed forms I had received to that date. It was not a big sample, but we felt that they would give us at least an indication of whether I was moving on the right lines. There might even be some pointers of what direction I should take in the future.

Charlotte's analysis, dated 1 October 1990, revealed a wide range of individual responses and, as so often happens in research when a solution is not clear cut, it raised a host of new questions. Charlotte listed five; two of these especially interested me – 'What is/are the key therapeutic element(s) of the interaction?' and 'Who in particular can experience these benefits?' She ended the letter that accompanied the report with a comment that I could wholeheartedly endorse: 'There is much exciting work to be done!'

Dr Teasdale discussed dolphin therapy with a colleague, Dr Paul Gilbert, the author of *Human Nature and Suffering*, who had a deep interest in psychobiology and its relevance to the treatment of depression. Could it be, Dr Teasdale wondered, that a dolphin's lifestyle was an extreme form of what Gilbert had defined in primates as the 'Hedonic Mode' in which the social structure of a group was one of mutual dependence? It was marked by reassurance signals, allowing safer exploration of the social environment – as in mother-child interactions. When threatened, the child will seek out the mother, who reassures her offspring by stroking, holding and cuddling. In his book Paul Gilbert writes:

Associated with the *hedonic mode* (my italics) of social interaction is an accentuation of co-operative behaviour, especially exploration and problem solving. Chimpanzees often split into small groups for foraging. Hence the social behaviours arising from the hedonic mode are basically those of confidence giving, mutual support and reassurance. These are quite different, indeed the exact opposite of those of the *agonic mode* (my italics) in which the styructure of the social organisation is based on dominance and defence . . . Chance believes that it is the hedonic mode which has been the spur to creative human intelligence. In the hedonic mode, the attentional capacity is more open and allows for different inputs to be integrated. . . . Furthermore, in terms of psychotherapy, Chance suggests that it is only by operating in the hedonic mode (which involves reducing arousal) that change and growth of personality can take place. All the time a person remains in an agonic (defensive) state, there is restriction of attention and a limited capacity for integrating new information.

Dr Teasdale suggested that dolphins were able to facilitate the hedonic aspect of ourselves rather than the more competitive mode of which we are all so capable. Here was a possible explanation for the effect of dolphins on the human psyche from two of Britain's most respected research workers in the field who looked at my data with the cool eye of objective scientists.

A similar conclusion was reached by Rebecca Fitzgerald who lives in New Mexico. In 1985 dolphins appeared to her in a series of dreams and instructed her to write down their messages – which she did. Each morning afterwards she awoke full of exuberance and joy, with more energy than she had had for years.

Two years went by. Rebecca finished graduate school, did her internship in hospital, ran the out-patient therapy group and developed a private practice in psychotherapy in Santa Fe. She should have been all set for a predictable career but instead had a powerful sense that she was doing the wrong thing. Then one day she saw in a Jungian journal a picture of Dr Betsy Smith working with autistic children and semi-captive dolphins.

'I took one look at the big Bottlenose dolphin called Fonzie and thought my brain would explode,' she told me some years later. 'I straight away telephoned Betsy and found out how to swim with the dolphins in Florida.'

While continuing to give lectures and to run her private clinic, Rebecca set up Dolphinswim, an organisation through which she could introduce people to the healing power of dolphins. After several trips to the Florida Keys she had another visitation from the same spotted dolphins. This was followed for several nights in a row with dreams in which she re-experienced good and nurturing events from her childhood. Finally, waking with a start, she said out loud: 'Who is doing this?' Then, fully alert, she heard them tell her that in her conscious hours she had been focusing on only the painful part of her childhood, and that actually people *choose* their memories.

'There was a long silence,' she said, continuing her story. 'Then I heard them say very clearly – "choose again".'

Rebecca's choice was to take her next Dolphinswim group to Great Bahama Bank - a region of shallow, warm, crystalline water between the coast of Florida and the Bahamas which was frequented by schools of dolphins – not Bottlenose dolphins (*Tursiops truncatus*), such as those with which she had swum previously, but *Stenella plagiodon*, otherwise known as Spotted dolphins. Here is the account she sent me:

I was fortunate enough to be the only passenger awake the first morning at dawn. We'd passed the first night in a big storm and everyone else was finally getting some sleep after being tossed around all night. I woke up about 5.30 and was completely alert. I felt compelled to get out of my bunk and go up on deck. In the distance, several shining black dorsal fins were streaking directly towards our vessel. I slid quietly into the water. I could see the dolphins were speckled, just like those in my dreams. As I rolled, dove and spiralled up and down through the turquoise water they kept exact pace with me. The synchronicity of our movement was effortless. I felt I was born to do just this. Suddenly two adult dolphins pulled up beside my head, one hovering over the other. They gently nudged me and looked deep into my eyes.

Within my mind I formed the question, 'Are you the dolphins who came in my dreams?' No sooner did I form the last word of the question than they zoomed straight up out of the water, doing leaps and spins and somersaults. They swam in tight circles around me, the water absolutely pulsing with sound. I felt I would *explode* with joy! I became another creature entirely. I held my breath for long periods and felt the water course over my body in a way I'd never felt before. I swam with a power and grace and energy that I'd never known to be possible.

From that moment Rebecca knew precisely what she had to do next in her life. She would give as many people as possible the opportunity to experience the joy and liberation she had found in the Bahamas.

'But how do you think it works?' I asked her.

'Most people describe that ecstatic physical feeling as a sensation of *coming home*', she said. 'I believe that is because we are, in our most basic state, joyous, creative, powerful beings. Our wholeness resides within us; the trick is to access it. The dolphins are somehow able to assist us in experiencing it for ourselves.'

John Hunt, a solicitor practising in London arrived at a different explanation based upon his own personal experiences. The sensitivity of whales and dolphins always fascinated him and this led to a personal encounter with Funghie in 1989.

In Dingle he met a group from London and told them he wanted to set up a centre to educate people about dolphins as well as to learn from them. Fresh out of the sea and imbued with the uninhibited joy and optimism that comes only after a swim with a dolphin everyone said it was a splendid idea.

There and then they agreed to form an organisation, and the Dolphin Circle charity was born.

After a year or two Dolphin Circle was being called upon to comment on various dolphin issues. One day John found himself being interviewed on Breakfast Television after a film clip showing me swimming with Freddie in Amble. When asked what he thought about the healing effect of dolphins, John said he regarded dolphins as the extra-terrestrials with which we are most familiar. The interviewer was taken aback. The solicitor quickly pointed out that he was using the word literally, for the Oxford Dictionary definition of terrestrial is 'pertaining to the land of the world' – as distinct from the waters. He was not referring to dolphins as creatures from outer space. Still it was inferred from John's response that the true explanation might well hover on the limits of most people's credibility.

In a more direct answer to the question of healing, John Hunt went on to say that he didn't really know what the mechanism was – but was open-minded. One possibility was that dolphins could deliver exquisitely fine sonar beams into the hidden recesses of the human body. Perhaps one day, he continued, we would become intelligent enough to under- stand dolphin language and their intricate world of social interplay. Maybe it wasn't the kind of clear-cut answer that the viewers might have wished for. But to see and hear a well- respected professional man with a trained legal mind express such ideas had impact. It gave confidence to others who secretly harboured similar radical views and gave them the courage to express them openly.

The Dolphin Circle was just what was needed at a time when many long-established practices, ranging from medi- cine to the keeping of animals in cages, were under the microscpe. Most of their meetings were held in Regent's Park College, which ironically was a short distance from London Zoo – an out-moded institution on the verge of bankruptcy and desperately in need of a radical re-think. Members of Dolphin Circle were strongly opposed to dolphinariums.

The Circle was represented at the Bellerive Conference on

Captive Cetacea in Geneva in July 1989, and it was there that the dream of a release programme for captive dolphins, known as *Into the Blue*, became a reality. For the next two years John worked closely with Zoo Check (later to become the Born Free Foundation) on the legal side, battling against the opposition of the dolphinarium industry. The grand finale came on 10th September 1991 when he witnessed the happy release of Rocky, Missie and Silver in the Caribbean. Earlier these three dolphins had been flown from Britain and rehabilitated in a lagoon on the Island of Providenciales in the British West Indies. On a blustery day he watched them finally being let loose in open water. Seeing the dolphins roam once more ecstatically free made all the months of anguish and legal wrangling worthwhile.

But that was only the beginning of what, for John, turned into a fifteen month sojourn around the world. The next leg took him to Peru, where he worked with Roxanne Kremer and the Pink Amazon River Dolphin Foundation. Swimming with the delicate pink dolphins was made only slightly hazardous by the presence in the water of the dolphins' regular diet – piranha.

From there he travelled through Hawaii, Australia and Bali, finally arriving in Kaikora, New Zealand. There the round-the-world whale-watcher had a close encounter with the largest-brained inhabitant of our planet – a super-dolphin – the Sperm whale. He witnessed two specimens oxygenating with twenty-five consecutive blows on the surface before sounding. Shortly afterwards he had one of the greatest moments of his life.

'Suddenly my vision was filled with the sight of a Humpback whale breaching out of the water and thundering back with a slow-motion splash,' John told me shortly after his return. I asked him if his trip had shed any new light on the healing power of dolphins.

He surprised me by saying: 'Dolphins are wise. Wisdom is to do with understanding the interconnectedness of all things. Somewhere in that understanding occurs true healing.'

Dreams and *transformation* were words that cropped-up frequently when I questioned people who had come under the spell of dolphins. As a child Annalisa Solla was very pessimistic about life and what she saw as the inevitable end that would befall the human race through greed and selfishness. One day she bought a secondhand book, a fictional story about some dolphins who communicated telepathically with children. After she had read the book and traded it in Annalisa started to dream about dolphins. Slowly the idea took hold that the dolphins and what they stood for would be one of several guides that would lead man away from self-destruction. She thought most people would regard it as a harebrained notion. It was not until her early twenties that Annalisa felt comfortable enough to speak openly about it. To her surprise most friends were sympathetic to the idea, and even encouraged her to follow her intuition.

In January 1992 Annalisa produced an audio visual presentation as part of her degree course at the University of Westminster. She used it to communicate her feelings about dolphins through pictures and sounds. She included mythology, telepathy and the births of humans underwater in the presence of dolphins. She contacted me and told me she felt the audience was picking up something positive from her dolphin images. I was immediately reminded of some feelings Tricia Kirkman had expressed to me some years earlier, shortly after she had visited the National Portrait Gallery in London.

Tricia had found herself bursting with excitement as she stood and looked at the paintings, feeling so much passion she could hardly contain herself. She could not understand why everyone around her seemed so unaffected. They appeared to be completely unaware of the powerful emotions that she could feel emanating directly from the paintings. The experts were talking gobble-de-gook, seriously taking notes and earnestly discussing prices. To Tricia, everything was secondary to the unseen force that came from the pictures and touched her heart.

'So there you are,' I said to Annalisa, having told her how

sensitive Tricia was, 'I am sure art can capture and project an essence and feelings.' Later Annalisa wrote to me:

> Dolphins have acted as a catalyst for a transformation in myself. In my dreams the dolphins spoke and gave me the strength and the determination I so desperately needed. Looking back, it seems a long time ago when I believed that the best way out of this existence for mankind was self-destruction. Pessimism has turned full way and I am now optimistic.
>
> This leads me to my third year project. I want to alert the general public to the more mysterious side of dolphins. What better medium than art? I want to organise an exhibition, *The Healing Potential of Dolphins*. It is the result of eight years struggle, confrontation, fear and ecstasy with the belief that dolphins in some way or other can help man regain his life and live it, not just exist. This idea is connected with the Gaia principle and I often get the impression that I am being used as an instrument by this energy.
>
> For me dolphins signify a future that is bright; however, to reach it we must be ready to trust ourselves, and our intuitive feelings.

Annalisa told me she had found her project extremely challenging. It had made her face up to her innermost feelings. I also discovered that she had never seen a free dolphin. Yet through dreams the dolphins had enabled Annalisa to move from a state of pessimism to a joyous and creative optimism.

John Farrar painted dolphins, usually in association with his other passion – sailing ships. Although English, John lives in Edam in Holland, where he has made a living as an interior designer. He suffered from bouts of acute hyper-ventilation and hoped the *Dolphin Dreamtime* tape would help him relax and control his breathing. He found listening to the tape put him into a state of deep relaxation in which he had profound but pleasant experiences. Later he tried to rationalise what was happening to him and wrote this letter to me:

> I got an instant feeling of relaxation going down the steps

into the cave. Being in a cave has a safe feeling, and, reading Bruce Chatwin's book *The Songlines*, I feel that it must be an inherited feeling from our ancestors who took refuge in caves. The crystals did not quite work on me; I could find no significance – but I could imagine flame reflections dancing on the cave walls and on crystals.

Instead of a beautiful garden I imagined I was in a jungle. There again I felt like prehistoric man or Tarzan.

I went into the water with the dolphins, which is easy to imagine, but I could only picture dolphins from films which I have seen on TV. The feeling of swimming in water is very relaxing. The dolphins took me to a cave with prehistoric caveman paintings of animals on the walls. I tried to imagine being a dolphin swimming underwater. It must have worked because when I returned back into the room I suddenly felt like opening a can of herrings.

The third time I listened to the tape I imagined I was a dolphin and was breathing through the top of my head. I could in fact feel the tubes opening from the back of my nose to my ears and up to the top of my head. It did not feel at all strange. I imagined I was swimming with other dolphins in the sea and I had a picture from the air looking down onto myself as a dolphin. I thought about people having out of body experiences. I had had one myself while in hospital after I had been given sleeping pills. I looked down on myself in bed, then flew off through the window.

It suddenly occurred to me that maybe dolphins had a kind of out of body vision, so that they could see where they were in relation to the coastline, like a radar screen built from their sonar but much more sophisticated than watching a TV screen. By using the data from their sonar, or songlines as used by Aboriginals, they could perhaps achieve an out of body 3D picture, as if seen by a bird flying overhead, looking down on themselves and the outlying coastline and reefs and islands, like a kind of dream in 3D, to fix their location and the location of food.

You could then assume that, if this intelligence was

taken to its ultimate, they could travel anywhere they wished in and out of body vision or awareness. And it would be possible to communicate with humans who inherit a similar sense but do not now use it.

Bruce Chatwin thought that men may also have had a kind of sixth sense to locate their position while travelling or migrating. It's an interesting idea, and it makes our radar and sonar look very primitive.

I then hit on an idea while watching TV. If a strong magnet or electronic force field interference interrupts the radio wavelengths the picture becomes distorted or pulled to one side. So, if dolphins used a picture made up electronically and there was a sudden change in the Earth's magnetic field or some radio interference occurs, then their 3D picture or dream would also be distorted. This could account for both dolphins and whales being stranded on beaches.

As a painter I know it is possible to visualise a picture clearly in your head, then try to put it down on paper in a painting.

I also know that the more relaxed you feel the more you are stimulated to receive these pictures.

My thought and memory is made up from pictures in my mind. I picture a word before I can write it down. That's why I am a bad speller. I can picture a person but cannot remember their names, so already we can say that this is possible in dolphins also.

I enclose some slides of my recent paintings that were produced from this pre-imagined picture process.

Yours faithfully,
John Farrar

Had I received John's letter before the events I am about to relate I might have logged the ideas in my mind, filed the letter and thought little more about it. When it arrived early in 1992, it made me wonder once again if the artist and the poet are not more perceptive than the scientist whose mind is so often fenced in by education and training.

· 13 ·

The Cortona Experience

If you take a professor of theoretical physics, a Zen Master, a Japanese calligrapher, a Viennese baroque ensemble, an Indian philosopher, a Hawaiian healer, a German sculptor, an American neurologist, a French author, a political historian, an expert on genetic engineering, a couple of management experts, two Italian geologists, an assortment of highly talented artists, a mixture of musicians, a professor of psychology, stir in a handful of therapists, add a splash of dolphins, put them in a monastery in a medieval town on a hill in Tuscany, let loose a hoard of aspiring graduates and doctorates, tell them to sort out metamorphosis in a series of lectures, discussions and workshops and nourish them on Italian food and wine, then you may get some idea of what happened to me in Cortona during a week in April 1991.

Naturwissenschaft und die Ganzheit des Lebens or 'Science and the Whole of Life' were the official titles of the event which everyone referred to as the Cortona Conference. Its name alluded to the small medieval town in Italy where it took place. This extraordinary mind-stretching gathering was the brainchild of Professor Pier Luigi Luisi of Eidgenössische Technische Hochschule in Zurich who found a Swiss benefactor to underwrite most of the costs.

Professor Luisi saw the narrow confines of the scientific mind as one of the sources of the problems besetting present-day civilisation, which is largely shaped by the activities of scientists. The Cortona Conference was not intended as an initiative against science, but to promote the nurture of better scientists, or scientists who were more aware of the

'Ganzheit (whole) of Life', as he called it. The programme, intended primarily for young Swiss scientists, was based on the idea that academic education, although technically useful, was in danger of producing hi-tech specialists who lacked an understanding of the broader issues of life. It aimed therefore to present a renaissance of spiritual and humanistic values within a scientific framework.

The Conference took place in a monastery which doubled as a hotel and conference centre. The Hotel Oasi, which was set between silver-barked olives and ancient cypresses, enjoyed secluded gardens with panoramic views over the Tuscan countryside.

When I accepted the invitation to participate I had no idea what I was letting myself in for. It turned out to be the starting point of a new dolphin trail, a road that would lead me back to Australia and into a new situation more bizarre than anything I had experienced before. Furthermore, it directly involved the Japanese – the last people on earth from whom I expected help or inspiration in my quest for the source of the healing power of the dolphin.

I was a last-minute addition to the conference programme and assumed my role was to add a nosegay of dolphins into the heady mix. I gave my presentation in a chapel. When I was not performing, I took the opportunity – under the guidance of the renowned sculptor, Willi Gutman – to create a sculpture incorporating the elements of life: wood, iron, stone, fire and water. When I wasn't chipping away at my piece of stone or forging a bar of iron, I watched, painted and engaged in animated debates. I was pleased to be able to discuss with Dr Clifford Saron, from the Department of Neuroscience at the Albert Einstein College of Medicine in New York, his observations on brain development and related them to my theories on dolphin intelligence.

In his presentation Clifford Saron showed some remarkable film sequences at high magnification of a growing chick brain. They revealed migrating growth cones moving very selectively towards the position they would finally occupy in a neurite, which in turn would find its own specific location in the organised structure of the chick's brain. A similar chain of events undoubtedly also took place in the growing human brain, eventually resulting in what we considered to be the ultimate independent intelligence. But was it? What if we were just the equivalent of individual brain cells that were linked in some way to be part of a higher global intelligence beyond our limited comprehension? Clifford Saron pointed out that, even if this was not the case in the past, we are now at a stage when such a global brain does physically exist, with computers providing the network necessary to link the components together.

Furthermore, the global human-based brain is growing at an exponential rate as computer technology advances. Most young people in the Western world are becoming computer literate.

I already had direct knowledge of one result of the global brain through my son Ashley, who was pioneering the concept of harnessing the telephone network, fax machines and computers to enable people to work from home or in remote locations. He told me that 70 per cent of those using flat paper no longer needed to travel long distances to work. Communication and technology enabled many people to work in pleasant rural situations without the drudgery or the pollution of commuting.

Part of Clifford's presentation concerned a journey he and a group of colleagues had made to India to see the Dalai Lama, a winner of the Nobel Peace Prize. There they each gave a presentation in their respective fields of research in the brain. What had surprised them was the alacrity with which His Holiness understood their topics and posed the very questions which they themselves were asking, and which were leading them to new horizons of discovery.

It so happened that I had met the Dalai Lama during a brief visit he made to England a month before the Cortona Conference. To this day I do not know why I was invited to the reception, or why the Dalai Lama chose to talk to me in the throng. But this he did, signifying his intention by holding my hand throughout our conversation, which was about the similarity of the current position of the whales and dolphins to that of the Tibetans.

The slaughter and present plight of the whales and dolphins has been well documented in books such as *Whale Nation* by Heathcote Williams. Decimation reached a peak in about 1950, the year when the Chinese invaded Tibet and began their reign of genocide. More than a million died, and thousands were moved into labour camps. Most of the temples were destroyed. The Dalai Lama, along with about 100,000 refugees, was forced to flee in 1959 to Dharamsala in India, where his headquarters has been ever since. From there the Tibetan leader, who is regarded by his followers as the reincarnation of the Buddha of Compassion, preaches non-violence, convinced that one day the Tibetans will get their land back.

Clifford and I agreed that our respective meetings with the Dalai Lama had left each of us with an abiding sense of his wisdom and serenity in adversity. He had spoken gently, with humour and without rancour, of his sympathy for the ill-conceived needs of the invaders.

One evening towards the end of the conference Clifford's wife, the cellist Barbara Bogaton, gave a recital in a chapel with a vaulted ceiling under the monastery. After performing a Bach sonata Barbara started to create sounds spontaneously. In addition to plucking the strings of her cello, she used her bow to tap the legs of her chair and the heating pipes behind her. The Baroque Ensemble, all in period costume and playing medieval instruments, joined in. A pianist raised the lid of a grand piano and started to pluck the strings with his fingers. Then Carlo Testa (from Zurich) fed paper from a huge roll into the audience and handed out crayons and paints. Everyone took part in an orgy of artistic creativity. All the barriers of conformity were down.

Earlier in the week a group reported on a visit to Japan. In association with some of the Japanese delegates present they wrote and performed a witty sketch in which they depicted and debunked a day in the life of a Japanese businessman. Humour was a side of the Japanese that I had never come across before. When I attended a workshop on 'Calligraphy as a Healing Art', I was introduced to a spiritual dimension of Japanese culture. It was run by Shizuko Ouwehand, who dispelled the dislike I had harboured of the Japanese nation since my childhood days when Britain was at war with Japan and I was indoctrinated with the view that we were defending ourselves from a callous and barbaric race.

Shizuko, about the same age as me, was born in Kito. If she had been instilled with similar feelings against the British and the Americans for dropping an atomic bomb on Hiroshima, she had long since abandoned them. She was active, alert and alive. Her gait was typically Japanese. She walked with a rapid succession of short steps that made her passage, which was always graceful, look like a speeded-up movie. She was deeply emotional but, unlike many Japanese, did not keep her feelings hidden behind an inscrutable expression.

A joyful inner energy bubbled up in Shizuko, especially when she was in company. This sometimes veiled the deeply sensitive person that also lurked within and was concerned for the well-being of all her fellow humans. Her face was a transparent window through which her emotions sometimes shone so clearly that it was hardly necessary to understand the words she spoke in order to comprehend the ideas and thoughts she was attempting to convey. Although this made her vulnerable, it was a considerable asset in her work as an interpreter in Japanese, Dutch, German and English, which she enjoyed immensely. For Shizuko was a natural communicator whose facility with languages enabled her to link up with a network of contacts that spanned the globe. Many of them were in the arts, as was her husband, a retired professor who was an expert on the Dutch Masters, including van Gogh. It was Shizuko's interest in Japanese art and religion that had brought the two of them together. She had taught Japanese calligraphy at Zurich University from 1968 until 1975. By that time she had begun her studies of Chinese astrology; she also realised the healing power of Japanese calligraphy if it was performed without any inhibitions.

Making the ink and splashing it joyfully on Japanese paper, becoming one's own brush, was her method of getting the participants at Cortona, myself included, to discover their inner depths.

The daily format of the conference was that all participants attended the two morning lectures and then, after lunch, people were free to attend or conduct workshops and discussion groups. Several of these were run concurrently and the choice was left to the individual. This arrangement meant that Shizuko, who ran a workshop every afternoon, was unable to attend the one discussion group on dolphins over which I was to preside.

Just before my morning session came to a close, Shizuko stood up and told everyone that the whales and dolphins were of great concern to her; indeed so important was it for her to come to my discussion group that she proposed to cancel her calligraphy workshop. Her class was a very popular event to which the numbers admitted were limited. Shizuko knew that to those who were looking forward to attending it would be disappointing. She asked the participants who had signed up to forgive her, and requested that they all came to my discussion group instead, and she would try to fit them in later.

It was Shizuko who introduced me to 'Ki' (pronounced Kee and sometimes spelt 'Chi', or 'Qi'), the force that keeps the body in a harmonious state. She told me that she worked closely with a man called Nakagawa, who had cured many people in Japan and in other parts of the world with Ki. Nakagawa had had many honours bestowed upon him, including an honorary professorship from the University of Honolulu. The more we discussed my work with dolphins and Nakagawa's work with Ki, the more obvious it became that I should meet him – but when, and how?

Destiny had that matter sorted out, I told Shizuko. I had already embarked on a dolphin trail that could possibly lead me to Tokyo. The route began in Amble and my first tentative steps along it took place in August 1989 when I introduced Michael Heinrich to Freddie the dolphin.

· 14 ·

In Touch with JoJo

Michael Heinrich was tall, of medium build, and his thick blond curly hair had the merest hint of auburn. His skin was fair. He had a disarming smile, radiated a gentle sensitivity and had an air of quiet self-assurance.

He had come to Amble to see Freddie and me. We wandered to the end of the jetty to look out for the dolphin. Conditions were not perfect. We discussed the situation and decided Michael should go in. There was no urgency. He kitted-up in his wetsuit and finned away from the steps towards a group who were already in the water hoping for a dolphin encounter.

There was considerable excitement when Freddie's dorsal fin arrived in the middle of the harbour entrance. It was followed by a lot of noisy slapping of fins on the surface as the swimmers rushed off towards the dolphin. Michael waited, just hovering quietly in the water. A few moments later, when all the others were scattered over a wide area in their attempts to catch him, Freddie the dolphin appeared beneath Michael. White belly uppermost, the dolphin was watching the human looking down at him. When Freddie made it obvious that he wanted to be stroked, Michael extended his arm gently and felt the dolphin's smooth rubbery skin with his hands, allowing them to slide over the surface as Freddie moved. I had seen it happen often before. With half a dozen people in the water to choose from, Freddie chose which one he wanted for company, and on this day he stayed with Michael despite the desperate enticements the others were making. When they started to close in Freddie decided it was time to disperse the group. He visited most of the swimmers in turn, all of whom chased after him when he appeared nearby. He soon had them spread around the jetty before going back to Michael who remained quietly waiting for Freddie to return.

That evening I discovered, to my surprise, that Michael had never worn a wetsuit or the other equipment before. He had put them on confidently, without any fuss, and I had assumed he was at least familiar with them, even if he wasn't an experienced diver. It was easy for Michael – or appeared to be. His life was like that, and always had been. He didn't have to work hard to pass exams. So he spent much of his time skipping school and cycling round the Surrey country-side, studying the old buildings which fascinated him. In the evenings, instead of doing homework, he ran a rock band. Technical subjects posed no problems for him, and with a natural flair for languages he became polylingual.

When Michael left school, he decided against architecture as a career, and went into the commercial world where he made a lot of money acting as a business consultant, as well as making film and television commercials. Sometimes he ran as many as five film crews simultaneously, some of them working behind the Iron Curtain. He had a large house in Sussex and two lovely children. Everything was rosy, but then again it wasn't. He felt guilty that he could earn more in a month than his father, who was a highly skilled engineer, could earn in a year. His marriage broke up. He was close to a nervous breakdown.

Fascinated by the possible existence of an alternative intelligence, with a code of behaviour and perhaps even a morality with which he could relate, Michael decided to explore the possibility of making contact with a dolphin. Hence his presence in Amble.

I told him that I was due to give a film show the following evening in the Lake District and invited him to come along. The show was a condensed version of my many years of experience with dolphins. I felt it would provide a good platform from which he could launch his own rocket into the nebulous realms of the dolphins, if that was what he eventually decided to do. And the omens were good.

Michael was not the sort of person who wanted to clock up hundreds of hours of dolphin swims. He had enjoyed his swim with Freddie and felt a definite affinity with whatever it was that made dolphins so attractive to humans. But what next? Although Freddie was possibly the friendliest wild dolphin in the world, I told Michael that earlier in the year I had been to the island of Providenciales in the British West Indies where I had met Dean Bernal and a friendly wild dolphin named JoJo. The relationship between JoJo and Dean was a quantum leap ahead of anything I had seen or experienced before.

Dean was physically super-fit, a very spiritual person, and in the clear warm waters of the Caribbean could, and did, spend many hours swimming with JoJo. Sometimes they would swim together from the beach out to the fringing reef over a mile offshore. There they would explore the drop-off together. Putting the tip of his beak into Dean's cupped hand, the dolphin would dive, towing Dean with him. They would often reach depths of more than thirty metres before they returned to the surface for air. When JoJo became infected with a barb from a Sting ray, Dean became very concerned for the well-being of his companion and sought veterinary advice. An antibiotic treatment was prescribed, and Dean managed to place the pills directly into the dolphin's stomach. Such was the closeness between them that he was able to open JoJo's teeth-lined jaws, insert his hand, and push it down the dolphin's gullet into the stomach cavity before releasing the antibiotic tablets. The sick dolphin did not take kindly to this abuse of trust, but Dean communicated that it was done with the very best of intentions and their relationship remained unimpaired when JoJo eventually made a full recovery.

What passed between Michael and Freddie when they were together off Amble I am not sure – and I don't think Michael is either. Whatever it was, Michael decided to set off on his own journey to explore the more spiritual aspects of the human/dolphin connection. Having heard my account of Dean and JoJo, the island of Providenciales stood high on his list of ports of call. He would need a pilot to steer his ship into these unknown waters, of course, and I could think of no one better suited to the task than – yes, you've guessed it – me!

To finance the trip, Michael arranged a business lunch in Milan at which, for a consultation fee, we produced some ideas for the launch of a new product.

We didn't really need an excuse for going to see JoJo other than to enjoy ourselves – but my conscience wouldn't let me do that. So I appeased it by agreeing to shoot some video film for John Levy with whom I had made the television programme *The Dolphin's Touch* about the Dingle dolphin. I also arranged to record some material for Mark Jobst for a BBC Radio programme. Everything was arranged for an 11.30 take-off from Heathrow on 23 October 1989.

We timed our departure so that we would not have too long to wait before we boarded the flight to Miami. Our luggage, tape recorders and boxes of camera gear were all stacked on a trolley in the hall of Michael's London flat on the morning of departure. I went out into the lobby to call the lift while Michael collected his post. As he did so the door to his flat swung shut and locked. Michael's coat and keys were inside, so was all of our baggage. We were outside. There was no caretaker. Everything we needed for our trip was behind the locked door. It was early in the morning.

What could we do? We could break open the front door, but could we leave it in that state, unsecured? It would have to be repaired afterwards. Michael had recently moved in and knew none of his neighbours. He aimed a karate kick at the door, and it flew open. The Yale lock was undamaged. We gathered our load and left, Michael locking the door as we departed.

Upon arrival at the island of Providenciales (or Provo, as it was commonly called) we negotiated for accommodation in a luxuriously appointed self-catering apartment at the

Ocean Club in Grace Bay, next to the Club Mediterranee. The beach directly outside our veranda was one of JoJo's favourite haunts. All we had to do was to sit in the sun under the palm trees and wait for him to turn up, which is no bad thing to do if you can think of it as work.

All the same, living out this ideal had its darker side – the yin and yang of life if you like. Some people were finding it difficult to cope with the personal and political conflicts that JoJo had introduced into their lives. The trouble arose largely from the fact that human society had become obsessive about ownership. If a person or a group owned a boat, or a house, or a piece of land, everyone knew where they stood and could argue, in a court of law if necessary, what it was worth and who should get any revenue the asset generated. But who owned JoJo? What was he worth to the economy of the island? Who had the film rights in JoJo? Who decided when JoJo was being unduly pestered by film crews and photographers? What should or could be done about it?

JoJo sometimes tipped people off water skis, not to mention that he had been known to hook people – females especially – with his penis. Such behaviour could, and did, cause havoc in diving classes in which people had dedicated themselves to the serious business of achieving aquatic proficiency. So what about the humans who were pestered by JoJo? Who could be sued for compensation?

As a dolphin expert I was expected to be able to answer all these questions instantly. Having already shown that dolphins could help those suffering from depression, I was well aware that these creatures could touch the emotions with great intensity. JoJo brought out the best and the worst in people. Some became excessively protective, but the human trait JoJo most exposed in people was selfishness. A few wanted the whole world to know about their relationship with the dolphin – because it was by far the most important and emotional aspect of their lives – but they wanted JoJo for themselves, and took exception to others who diverted the dolphin's attention elsewhere. They usually justified this attitude by accusing all intruders of exploiting the dolphin. Some undoubtedly did. Just discussing the topic could cause the eruption of intense anger.

When one person seriously suggested that it would be better if JoJo was put down or confined to a dolphinarium rather than being subjected to exploitation in the sea, I realised how irrational the situation had become. Such reactions were not special to JoJo. They happened everywhere and every time a dolphin became friendly. An element of tolerance and understanding needed to be introduced.

In our philosophical moments, of which there were many, Michael and I decided that letting go of thoughts of exclusivity when it came to sharing love and affection was one of the more difficult lessons the dolphins had to teach us.

Dean was caught in the whirlpool of emotions too. He loved JoJo intensely and was delighted to share that love with anyone else he thought would be sensitive to JoJo's need for quiet moments and time to feed. He was pressured by film crews who had come to do a job and were going to get their footage come hell or high water. With people like me focusing attention on JoJo, these problems weren't likely to go away.

Another person who had a big slice of JoJo's affection was Tim Ainley. He was in a better position than anyone else on Provo to spend time with JoJo because he didn't live on the island. Tim, who spent much of his time just offshore aboard his catamaran *Beluga*, was a romantic who had given up city life in Canada, built a boat and sailed away to a tropical paradise, where he not only found the sun and the sea and pretty girls, he also found a dolphin. This dropout was urbane, brown as a chestnut, extremely fit and very good-looking. His emotional link with JoJo was profound, and one evening he regaled us with stories which were more spellbinding and improbable than fiction. He talked of dark moonless nights when JoJo would be swathed in thousands of sparkling phosphorescent stars. There was something about a pact between himself and JoJo whereby, no matter what the time of day or night when JoJo arrived, if the dolphin thumped his tender against the hull of *Beluga*, Tim would go overboard for a swim with the dolphin.

We were invited to spend a few days cruising on *Beluga* and were joined by Doug Perrine, a freelance photographer from Miami, and Gloria Stewart, a freelance journalist from London.

Throughout my previous visit to Provo a few months earlier the water had been as transparent as crystal and the sea flat calm. Tim was able to bring his boat close inshore, making it easy to climb aboard from the beach of white coral sand. When Michael and I came to board the *Beluga* the sea was crashing on to the beach. The water was like skimmed milk coloured pale blue. Tim anchored offshore, so that we had to wade out through the waves carrying our cameras and tape recorders above our heads. The island was catching the aftermath of a hurricane that had raged hundreds of miles away. In such conditions underwater filming was a waste of time. We set sail to see if we could find JoJo.

JoJo found us and trailed the *Beluga* as we searched for clearer water. It was a glorious sail. We settled for a pretty reef, but I had to be content to film the dolphin in far from perfect conditions.

Tim had some silver balls made by Mayan Indians. They were called celestial balls and generated a soft, tinkling sound when shaken. JoJo loved them. The dolphin was mesmerised when Tim performed an underwater juggling act which produced celestial music.

I stayed in the water filming JoJo's antics until the batteries in the video camera were spent. I also shot all of the film in my stills camera. It wasn't exceptional stuff, but I felt I had made a good start. I climbed back on board the *Beluga* while Dean and Tim went off with JoJo to explore another reef a short distance away. After a while a shout went up. A large shark had appeared.

Legend has it that dolphins will protect humans from sharks, and JoJo was living out the legend, ramming the shark with his beak and thumping it down on to the coral. Although bigger than JoJo, the shark was no match for the dolphin's superior strength. It tried to take off but JoJo wouldn't leave it at that. He continued to buffet the shark and drove it like a sheepdog towards the *Beluga*. By the time it reached the catamaran, the shark was only half-conscious and it sank to the bottom. The dolphin, eager to show off his prowess as a shark guard, poked it up to the surface by the anchor chain. Not content with that, the dolphin remained under the shark, keeping it on the surface while performing a lap of honour around the catamaran. There were shrieks from Gloria Stewart, who realised it would make a good story.

'Take a picture,' she yelled at me.

'I can't – I've run out of film.'

'Well, film it.'

'I can't – the batteries are flat.'

JoJo was obviously pleased with the electrifying effect his appearance with the shark had had on those on the *Beluga* and kept the shark nearby for five minutes while we all watched and ran around excitedly. Then I returned to the water and watched him, through my facemask, drive the luckless creature away from the *Beluga* into the misty blue haze.

The next day the sea conditions were no better. It was partially overcast. When clear of the clouds, the sun beamed down with ferocious intensity. Once again JoJo arrived as soon as we got under way, towing a new-style aquaplane, shaped like a Manta ray and called a Mantaboard. Anyone hanging on to its extended wing tips as handles was pulled through the water in a flurry of foam.

When we stopped, Tim went for a swim with JoJo. I enjoyed watching the two of them together in interspecies harmony. Tim was strong and graceful and seemed to flow through the water. Having unhitched the Mantaboard, he discovered that if he held it in front of him with outstretched arms it acted as a hydrofoil when he finned hard. Pumping vigorously with his legs, and keeping his fins in unison – the dolphin stroke – he swept through the water around me in a series of rolls and loops, as if he were flying an underwater stunt plane. JoJo could hardly contain his excitement and swooped and zoomed like a maniac sub-sea swallow around the reef and Tim. A small turtle swam past disconsolately.

Michael and I had come to understand each other pretty well. I felt at ease in his company and appreciated his sharp unmalicious sense of humour. We both enjoyed cooking and creating meals. There were times when he would take himself off with a book and it never occurred to me to inquire when he would return. When I needed a hand with the video camera, with which I was unfamiliar, he would appear by my side unobtrusively and together we would sort out whatever needed to be resolved.

It was not in my nature to let opportunities for filming or diving with a dolphin slip by. During breakfast on the third day Michael suggested we should consider giving the boat trip a miss and quietly digest what we had seen and done during the previous two days. So we filmed the *Beluga* as she passed by, her sails bellied by the wind, JoJo frolicking in the wake. When he returned Tim told me the underwater visibility was much improved and they had seen JoJo with an impressive school of barracuda. To my surprise, I had no regrets about staying behind and spending a lazy day around the beach, even though we failed to make contact with JoJo the following day.

The water stayed murky close inshore until our last day. On the final morning I got up before the sun rose and went into the sea for a last swim. Just as the rim of a tangerine sun peeped over the horizon JoJo came alongside me. The barely perceptible waves were refracting the rays through the limpid water on to the seabed where they played ceaselessly as ribbons of white light. While I swam JoJo gently pressed his body lengthwise against mine and we moved slowly in unison, celebrating the birth of a new day. I put my arm over his back and, for a short time, hugged him towards me as we continued forward. When I took my arm away, JoJo stayed alongside, pushing himself gently up to me. It was a journey of pure magic and profound peace that will remain with me for ever.

When I looked closely at JoJo's head, I noticed that the rippling patterns of white lights were actually composed of the colours of the spectrum. Luminous rainbow tassels were dancing across the dolphin's skin as he looked at me blissfully through half-closed eyes. We swam in utter contentment parallel to the beach. I noticed Michael standing silently on the shore, watching. I signalled to him to come in, and when he reached us, I left and quietly waded to the beach so that he could enjoy his own private communion with JoJo.

The sea was still as we flew out of Provo later that morning. The sun burned like a furnace from a cloudless sky of peerless blue, and with the water like glass, every feature of the seabed was clearly visible. The diving boats from Club Med were out in conditions that were as near perfect for underwater filming as could be imagined – altogether different from the choppy water and zero visibility that had greeted us the day we arrived.

I have no regrets about leaving. I am going home with far more than I came. A memory is lingering, floating in my soul. It is the mystical, mysterious, ethereal moment of sunrise. Buoyed up by warm caressing water, I am suspended in a sea of tranquil blue, feeling the pressure of a dolphin pressing himself against my skin as we glide forward together in harmony. I am both within myself and outside myself. I am not separate from the sun, the sea, and the sky. I am part of them. There are no boundaries. I am adrift in the space between fantasy and reality.

After we left Provo Michael fell in love with an American girl, Debra, whom he married two years later. They made a home on the Hawaiin island of Kauai where he took up painting.

· 15 ·

The Great Buddha of
Kamakura

During my childhood in the Second World War I was con-
ditioned to revile the Japanese. The stories I was told later by
those who had survived internment, or had worked on the
notorious railway that was central to David Lean's film
Bridge on the River Kwai, reinforced my attitude towards
them. My hostility was fuelled in the postwar years, when
the Japanese continued whaling despite the fact that they
were driving some species to extinction. It rose to a peak
when I saw a film of the sickening slaughter of hundreds of
dolphins by Japanese fishermen off the island of Iki in 1978.
There the dolphins were regarded as pests that were eating
rapidly diminishing fish stocks, and the fishermen were paid
a subsidy for each dolphin they killed. To the rest of the
world, it was obvious that over-fishing, not the dolphins,
had caused the decline.

The dolphin cull was an annual event, and in 1980 a young
American member of Greenpeace, Dexter Cate, risked his
life by taking a kayak into the area where the dolphins were
corralled before execution. Under cover of darkness, he cut
the nets and managed to persuade some of the condemned
prisoners to swim to freedom. Dexter spent three months in
a Japanese jail for his daring commando-style raid. I corres-
ponded with him when he was released and discovered that
he was not in the least bitter about his treatment or the attitude of the fishermen. It was a matter of education, he
insisted; direct confrontation would be counter-productive.
When later I met Dexter in 1988, I found him to be a slight,
gentle and spiritual person who, in a peaceful way, was still

trying to persuade the Japanese to change their attitude. There was little evidence that he was making any progress. While the rest of the world was observing a moratorium on whale hunting, they continued the killing under the guise of 'scientific whaling', which everyone knew was just a euphemism for whale hunting for profit.

It was with some caution, therefore, that I greeted Michael Heinrich in London shortly after our visit to JoJo. He was excited about a woman he had met who might help the dolphin cause in Japan. Michael asked me to supply him with one of the gold dolphin pendants that were sold by the International Dolphin Watch mail order shop, and he gave it to her as a gesture of faith in his judgement.

A few weeks later, after returning from a trip canoeing with Killer whales in Vancouver, Michael sent me a letter to which he had added a laconic handwritten note: 'The dolphin pendant is working brilliantly as a dolphin ambassador!' Then came the phone call from Tokyo. Mary Corbett said she would like to come and see me on her next visit to England. She wanted to launch the *Dolphin Dreamtime* tape in Japan!

When I collected her from the railway station, Mary told me that the dolphin pendant had been much admired and many people had commented on how much they liked dolphins. She said that, although whale and dolphin meat was still on sale, attitudes in Japan were beginning to change, especially among the young, many of whom were openly opposed to whaling.

Mary's mother was Japanese and spoke no English. Her father was American. She had spent her early years in Japan and went to university in the United States. Tall, vivacious and utterly charming, she seemed to have got the best of both worlds from her dual heritage. She spoke several languages and ran her own business in Tokyo, which was involved with various marketing activities. Equally at home in Paris, Athens or London, she was, I discovered later, a frustrated archaeologist. The dolphin thread she had found running through some of the ancient cultures fascinated her. The idea of taking an imaginary journey into the world of the dolphins through *Dolphin Dreamtime* captivated her.

Mary felt that minds were now sufficiently open, especially among the young, for a Japanese version of *Dolphin Dreamtime* to be a sound commercial proposition. So she had put the idea to the record company, Meldac, and they had agreed to market it as a compact disc provided Mary helped with the preparation of the sleeve notes and promotion.

The entire package was soon enticingly and tastefully put together. The front two-page spread of the accompanying booklet showed Dean gently and very touchingly kissing JoJo. It was my favourite picture showing the loving human/dolphin relationship at its most tender. Surely nobody would want to kill a dolphin, let alone eat it, if they got the message from my pictures.

'Horace, will you come to Japan to help launch *Dolphin Dreamtime?*' Mary asked.

Before my departure I was in a state of emotional turmoil. By the end of the non-stop flight from London to Tokyo's Narita Airport I felt as if my head was full of cotton wool. The arrangements had been made very quickly and in a hasty telephone call I told Mary the date and time of my arrival. She said she would try to meet me. Everything was left very loose.

As I cleared customs I prayed she would be there. I wheeled my trolley from one end of the arrivals hall to the other, scanning the sea of Oriental faces as I went. Once, twice, three times. Was she delayed? Or wasn't she coming? I had some Yen notes but no coins. I could not find anybody who spoke English. Using sign language, I got a man to give me some coins for the phone, but he declined to take my note. The public pay phones were unfamiliar to me and I tried to follow the pictorial instructions. But no matter what I did, I couldn't get through. I lost my money and could find nobody else with enough English to help me. I was in an alien land. I had one address in the middle of a metropolis which was totally incomprehensible to me. I had seen Clive James explaining on television how utterly impossible it was for a foreigner to find his way round Tokyo. I spoke no word of Japanese. The telephone didn't work, my brain didn't work, and I felt like a tortoise trying to cross a motorway.

Then in the fog that was my memory I recalled Mary mentioning the word 'limo'. Yes, that was it, 'limo'. Frantically I searched in my briefcase for the scrap of paper which had been by the telephone when she had called me. It was covered in other scrawled messages – but there, scratched in the corner, were the words 'Catch limo to Yokohama'.

I found a booking counter for limousines. The man understood enough English to know that I couldn't use the phone and offered to dial Mary's office number for me. When he did so I realised that, with the numb state of my brain, I had omitted the first o of the area code which is deleted when dialling internationally, as I had always done when calling her from England.

The girl who answered said that Mary was not in the office and suggested I should catch the limo to Yokohama. She would try to locate Mary and let her know I had arrived. I bought a ticket for the 'limo' and went outside to look for a stretched car of the type used at airports in the States. There were none. A large coach drew up by the 'limo' sign. With my befuddled brain it took some time before I realised that the *coach* was the 'limo'. I clambered aboard just as it was about to depart.

On the flight I had listened on my Walkman to a tape recording of Heathcote Williams reading his poem *Autogeddon*. It started with a view of the planet from outside, from which point it appeared that the earth was inhabited not by people but by automobiles that used humans to fulfil all their needs, to fill them with food when necessary and to take them to where they wanted to go. They were the prime inhabitants of the planet. Everything was secondary to the motor car. Even the precious ground was covered in concrete for their passage, and on the journey to Yokohama I felt as if I had arrived in Autogeddon.

We moved slowly, and with frequent stops, along a concrete highway populated entirely by automobiles. I looked at the drivers of the lorries who sat like robots, staring straight ahead, prepared to stop, start and change gear according to the needs of their master – the vehicle. Away from the congested motorway were factories, factories, and still more factories, buildings, pylons, electrical cables, but no people, only a few robots who could sometimes be seen moving from one automobile to another. Robots in grey uniforms and wearing white smog masks took money from the driver robots when they stopped at the toll booths. They were expressionless human machines for collecting money – the money needed to keep their juggernaut masters moving. Japan was living up to all the horrors I had imagined.

After an interminable journey the coach deposited me at a terminal in Yokohama. I heaved my baggage on to a trolley and pushed it inside. To my utter relief, there I saw Mary browsing at one of the counters. I felt like a lost child who had found its mother. A Catholic who had found the Virgin Mary herself could not have been more relieved. Mary gave me a hug and smiled – yes, she smiled. She was not a robot. She had emotions. My head was still fuzzy, but it didn't matter because I didn't have to use it. I could delegate everything to Mary until my brain started to function properly.

We drove through narrow streets with no pavements to her house. Some of the rooms were in the throes of redecoration. There were no electric lights in the bathroom. Mary told me she liked bathing by candlelight. There was food in the kitchen and an assortment of cats outside. They were fed by Mary's mother, who lived nearby. There was an old record player, a tape machine and a choice of music in which I could lose myself. I had a home. I was no longer an alien in an alien land.

Mary and her sister Evelyn introduced me to Japanese food, which I ate throughout my six-day stay. I was made an Honorary Member of the Foreign Correspondents Club of Japan where I gave an after-luncheon presentation that was to launch me and *Dolphin Dreamtime* into the public eye.

The media interviews and meetings with Mary's friends continued the process of changing my attitude to the Japanese that had begun in Cortona. The dozens of people I met socially and the thousands I saw crowded in the streets bore no resemblance to the slit-eyed, remorseless whale killers that had for so long hung like dark shadows in my mind.

The event which had the most profound effect on the manner in which I viewed the Japanese was a visit to Kamakura, about 50 km south of Tokyo and reached by a short train journey. It was the first time I had been aware of trees. Since my arrival machines, cars, trains and buildings had dominated my vision of Japan.

Leaving the station, we were soon climbing a densely wooded trail past magnificent temples and shrines that sat as naturally as standing stones in a forest. In medieval times Kamakura was the nation's capital.

I gazed in wonder at the massive wooden structures. The spiritual energy that pervaded the hillside reminded me of the Dingle peninsula and made me instantly aware that the Japanese had a long and powerful past. I could sense it. Unseen chanting monks added to the feeling that I had moved into a peaceful, strangely unearthly realm. We dallied in a formal garden based on Zen philosophy. Using subdued colours, and gravel carefully arranged in symmetrical modern designs which nevertheless dated back a thousand years, the gardeners had created a sense of infinity in a limited space. The primordial elements – wood, water, air and stone – were carefully arranged and blended to provide a symbolic microcosm of a wider order. It was not a place to romp through but a theatre of collective memory in which the spirits of the past were ever present.

For me, as a newly arrived westerner, here was a paradox – an oasis for peace and meditation in a country in which the work ethic had apparently gone berserk. Perhaps it was an ability to draw on this unseen spiritual force that enabled the Japanese to maintain an air of calm in the chaos and crowding in which the majority were forced to spend most of their lives, and which, in a place like New York, often erupted in violence.

Another illustration of the dichotomy of the Japanese character revealed itself when I watched a group of young women, dressed in long robes, participating in classical archery under the stern surveillance of an inscrutable, white-haired master with a goatee beard, who appeared to supervise the proceedings without making a single gesture. The girls, all tall, and holding aloft bows that were longer than themselves, stood like statues of classical Greek goddesses before very, very slowly pulling back the arrows and letting them fly. They did not look at the target. Instead they concentrated their minds on making the arrows go where they willed. Once they had fired, the archers remained still before very slowly lowering their bows. Then gracefully they left the stage upon which they were standing in line and floated together to form a group. When they saw me taking photographs they hid their faces behind their hands and burst into a fit of giggling, so reverting at once from deities to a gaggle of typical teenagers.

From the peace and tranquillity of the wooded hillside Mary, my guide, led me to the site of Kamakura's most famous monument – the Great Buddha. On the way we encountered a Shinto wedding procession. The bride and her attendants, attired in classical elegant kimonos, moved through the wandering crowds, many of them youngsters wearing faded and deliberately mutilated jeans – another contrast. Some of the throng wafted the smoke from special scrolls of smouldering paper over their bodies to clear away unwanted spirits. Others threw money into collecting boxes in the shrine. Afterwards they stood, still and erect, clapped their hands together, fingers straight and pointing upwards, before sharply nodding their heads in veneration.

The statue of the Great Buddha – the height of six men and weighing 100 tons – was cast in bronze in 1252.

Originally it was gilded and housed in a temple. But in 1495 a huge tidal wave, generated by a typhoon, swept in from the sea a kilometre away and destroyed the building. The statue remained unharmed. Now exposed to the elements, which have painted it with a grey-green patina, the Great Buddha is a link with a bygone age. Its imposing presence serves to remind those who come to gaze upon it that the religious faith that inspired it, and the skills of the craftsmen who built it, are still alive in Japan today.

I played my didgeridoo outside before going into the massive hollow casting. It was almost closing time, and everyone departed, leaving me alone inside. The sound of the didgeridoo is greatly influenced by the shape and nature of the surroundings close to the open end of the pipe. So I played my didgeridoo pointing it into hollows and revelling in the reverberating tones that swirled around the inside of the Buddha-shaped echo chamber.

· 16 ·

Dolphin Odyssey

I returned to Japan on 18 June 1991, just five weeks after my first visit, this time at the request of Professor Masato Nakagawa who had invited me to give a paper on dolphin therapy at his 100th Seminar on Natural Healing. The invitation came via Shizuko Ouwehand, who described herself as my 'Dolphin Playmate' and had remained in contact with me since the Cortona Conference. The timing was perfect, for it coincided with the opening of '*Dolphin Odyssey*' – an exhibition of dolphin art that Mary Corbett had organised in Tokyo's largest departmental store. I was booked into the Hotel Metropolitan in the centre of Tokyo.

The contrast between my first arrival at Narita Airport and the second could not have been greater. This time I was met by a member of Mary's staff. I was also returning to a country and a people with whom I now felt a certain affinity – a situation which I would have dismissed as absurd six months earlier.

On my previous visit I had seen that, in many ways, the Japanese had become extremely materialistic. Cars were usually scrapped after three years. The cost of a road-worthiness certificate, which required a complete strip-down, was more than £500. I was told this had been engineered by the car manufacturers to keep up the demand for new cars. Long before their working lives were over, television sets were also often thrown away, just for the sake of having the latest model. Conservation was not a word that sprang readily to Japanese lips.

In Tokyo property prices were astronomical, and rising.

Everyone seemed to be obsessed with working and spending. Here in the capital city there was very little outward appearance of the spiritual heritage I had seen when I visited the temples and the Great Buddha at Kamakura. At the same time, there was none of the tension I had experienced in Miami, for instance, or other cities in the West where rampant consumerism also ruled.

I was surprised to be told that I was the only presenter at Nakagawa's seminar and that I had been given the entire session which lasted three hours. I asked about a break, and Shizuko told me I could introduce one if I wished, but it wasn't usual practice. So I bombarded my audience non-stop, with Shizuko interpreting. She told me later that she had become so captivated by what I said that she often forgot the words. Instead of a precise translation, she presented my ideas in her own way, feeling no inhibitions. For me, it was tiresome to keep stopping for translation, but it spared the audience my habit of machine-gunning listeners with words. A few of those present could understand some English, most could not. Yet I sensed that they were appreciating our double-act. Indeed, afterwards one man who could speak English told me how brilliantly Shizuko had conveyed my message. 'You and Shizuko were like one,' he said.

Professor Nakagawa demonstrated his natural healing powers before I spoke. The force was said to radiate from his hands which, with fingers outstretched in the form of a five-pointed pyramid, he pointed at those present. He was accompanied for part of the time by music. The combination of the two sent some of the audience into what appeared to be a trance. Some rocked quietly from side to side with their eyes shut. Others waved their arms in the air like eastern dancers. One female member of the audience rose from her seat and, swaying like a snake, made her way to Nakagawa where she writhed at his feet. She was totally unaware of what she was doing, Shizuko told me. Nakagawa appeared to ignore her and went on 'treating' his audience by pointing his fingers. It was altogether bizarre. I was the only Westerner in a room filled with Eastern people who seemed to have left their bodies and gone into a state of ecstasy.

I have to admit that this sort of thing usually makes me feel distinctly uncomfortable. I can see no virtue in gullibility, nor in the leaders of quasi-religious sects mesmerising their flock into parting with money and themselves becoming rich in the process. I was to learn the following day that Nakagawa himself had come under scrutiny as a charlatan and had spent time in prison. Yet, oddly enough, I felt neither embarrassed nor uncomfortable in this crowded Japanese room in which such strange rituals were taking place.

After my presentation Nakagawa gave another of what looked to me like blessings. Once again the young woman rose from her seat and, with undulating and gyrating movements of her body, made her way to the front. She moved past Nakagawa and came to where I sat at a table. At first she waved her hands back and forth across the dolphin image on the sweatshirt I was wearing. Then briefly she held my hands before placing her thumb on a small pile of dolphin books I had stacked on the table in front of me, and pushing down on them with all her weight. The pile distorted and the top book slid down. Such was the force with which she pressed upon it that the book was slightly damaged. She continued to press until Nakagawa finished his treatment and swept his hand quickly across the top of her head, about six inches away from her hair. The movement brought her out of her trance and she walked back to her seat. Seeing my bemused expression, Shizuko explained to me that the lady in question was highly psychic and that what she was picking up was the Ki (pronounced Kee) force of the dolphins – not from me, not from the dolphin emblazoned across my chest, but from the words and pictures in my books.

At the end of the seminar I was introduced to members of the audience. I spoke to a dentist whose husband, a qualified doctor, had died of cancer. When she herself was given three months to live, she decided to abandon conventional treatment and rely for her survival on Ki. Three years later she was still alive, having written a book about her remarkable recovery. She was deeply moved by my account of Bill Bowell and the dolphins that had lifted his chronic depression after the best orthodox treatment had failed. To her, it seemed obvious that the dolphins were giving out the same kind of healing force that she herself had experienced.

I was surrounded by people who wanted to touch me and shake my hand. Although they were all smiling, many of them bore unmistakable signs on their faces that they had been through severe medical crises. To my surprise, several of them told me how much they supported my view that the killing of whales and dolphins should stop. Everyone here seemed to be convinced that dolphins had healing powers.

When it was all over the audience dispersed – in typical Japanese fashion – very quickly. The small group that remained retired to a nearby hotel, where we were joined by some Europeans for a traditional Japanese meal. Attentive women dressed in classical kimonos cooked food at the low table from which we ate and around which we attempted to sit cross-legged on the floor – a position which doesn't come without discomfort to those from Western societies with aging limbs. We drank saki from rare wooden cups, slurping the alcohol through small pinches of salt fingered into the corners of the wooden vessels. It was a noisy gathering, punctuated by complimentary speeches. Reluctant as I was, I added my own contribution. By the time I had finished I felt sure there wasn't one person in the room who did not wholeheartedly support all efforts to save the dolphins. I also said I would carry back to Britain with me the feelings of warmth and generosity I had experienced in Japan.

When the meal was over, I discovered that the night was still young in Nakagawa's eyes. We weaved through the crowds outside to one of his favourite bars, where he was warmly greeted by the hostess. The fact that we were stuffed with food and drink was of no consequence: another fine spread appeared before us. This smaller group, mainly Europeans, enjoyed the novelty of a Japanese bar that was uncompromisingly kitsch. A framed picture on the wall showed an illuminated waterfall which appeared to tumble down continuously. At the end of the bar was a video machine and two live microphones just waiting to be used. Nakagawa enjoyed singing, and with his vocal cords well lubricated with saki, he felt compelled to continue to entertain his guests with a Japanese song, accompanied by stereotyped Japanese scenes on the television screen. Tomes – rather like telephone directories – were handed round and we were all invited to find a song to sing. The words, in Japanese or English, were superimposed on bland pictorial sequences on a video.

Someone decided that my contribution should be Frank Sinatra's classic *My Way*, but when I looked up and saw the collection of grey men and the pink-tinted hair of the geriatric American women who frolicked across the screen and grinned at the camera with rows of immaculate white plastic teeth, framed in faces that were embellished with cascades of multi-coloured glass earrings, I could not bring myself to perform. I capitulated, however, when the next song came my way to the visual accompaniment of unclad nubile maidens cavorting demurely in a flower garden. I can't remember the name of the song, which was lost in a haze of saki.

The abrupt conclusion of my audition on Karaoke – a craze that has now swept across Europe – had an immediate effect on Nakagawa. He decided the night had ended. We all stood up as one, and departed. Shizuko wandered back with me to the Hotel Metropolitan.

'Sweet dolphin dreams, Horace,' she said, 'See you at the conference.'

'Do you want me to come?'

'Of course you must come. Everyone expects you. Nakagawa has made a special place.'

'Where's that?'

'You come to the reception. I meet you there.'

'What time?'

'Ten o'clock. Nakagawa would like you early in the programme.'

'You mean you want me to speak?' My surprise was drowned in saki.

'Yes, it's expected. All arranged. I am translating.'

I went to my room and have no further recollection until the telephone rang the next morning. The curtains were closed and it was still dark.

'Who is it?' I said in a sleepy voice, wondering who on earth could be calling me at four in the morning.

'Hello, Horace.' I heard Shizuko's chirpy Japanese voice. 'Are you coming downstairs? We are just about to start.'

I peered at the fluorescent numbers on the clock/radio beside me. It was gone five past ten.

'I'll be down in a few minutes,' I mumbled into the telephone before putting it down. Somehow, eight minutes later – washed, shaved and dressed – I wandered with as much nonchalance as I could muster into the reception room just as the presenters moved out to be received by the 300 delegates seated in the banqueting room.

All the arrangements for my visit had been made hurriedly on the telephone, without a confirming letter. Nobody had thought to mention my address to this august gathering of mainly Japanese, though also including delegates from twelve other countries, all dedicated to using and finding out more about Ki.

At the prescribed time of 10.15 precisely, and with Shizuko translating from Japanese into English and from English into Japanese, the Second Konoko-Shin-Atsu-Shin-Ryodo Symposium, as it was called, got under way.

Nakagawa started things off with a potted history of his work with Ki. The development of a machine he had invented to generate Ki was dealt with briefly before he launched into a detailed account of how it threatened the pharmaceutical companies and the medical establishment which had accused him of fraud. As a result, he had spent forty days in jail. Rather than languish in despondency, Nakagawa used his time to treat other prisoners who were ill, as well as the prison staff and their families.

The fact that so many people were prepared to attend a

conference in Tokyo added weight to his claims. I was certainly not in a position to comment on the effectiveness or otherwise of the use of Ki energy as a therapeutic tool.

Shizuko turned to me. 'It's your turn next, Horace.'

'What do you want me to talk about?'

'Just tell them what you told us yesterday!'

Before I could digest the concept of condensing a three-hour prepared presentation into a few minutes she ushered me on to the rostrum where my mind seemed to become disengaged from my body. I found myself reporting on Operation Sunflower and the benefits that dolphins could bestow upon those with mental illness. To link this with the main subject of the conference, I spoke briefly of the possibility that whales and dolphins were generating Ki and, if that were so, then they could play an important part in maintaining the planet in a healthy state. Removal or elimination of the whales by hunting, pollution, or invasive fishing techniques would be like eliminating white blood cells from the human body. I pointed out that the world was already showing signs equivalent to global cancer and that if we were unable to save the dolphins and whales we could be committing global suicide.

With tears of emotion running down her face Shizuko translated my message and we stepped off the stage to an ovation.

Nakagawa then reinforced what I had said about the importance of whales and dolphins and spoke of his own plans to work with them. He also said with a wry smile that he would have to be careful not to appear too contentious or he might be thrown into jail again. The Japanese had never agreed to abide by the worldwide ban on hunting whales.

I was impressed with the paper presented by Dr Joseph Brombach about his work using a therapy pool at a hospice in Germany. I also liked the irony of the Japanese possibly financing the world's first prototype dolphin therapy pool. So I arranged that the voluntary contributions made by the audience for Operation Sunflower should go directly to him to project dolphin sounds into his pool.

The congress came to an end with a group of young Japanese playing very heavy traditional drums which were set up on the stage. A teenage girl with sturdy legs attacked her drum using sticks thicker than broom handles with all the force her strong body could muster. Her performance was executed with the style of a master practising martial arts. She was the kind of person a mugger would do well to avoid.

Synchronicity is an attitude of mind in which it is accepted that when something important needs to happen all the events necessary for it to take place come together. You could say it was synchronicity that made it possible for me to introduce Nakagawa to the whole dolphin ethos. It also enabled me to attend Mary Corbett's 'Dolphin Odyssey' exhibition which opened at Loft Forum on the 12th floor of Ikebukuro Siebu Department Store on 19 June 1991. The show consisted of paintings, photographs and sculptures gathered from all round the world. The display included modern and classical art. Coral-white sand was carefully sculpted into classical Japanese symmetrical shapes. Sand, infused here and there with blue, was also moulded into asymmetrical forms to represent waves in the sea.

The feature that most captivated the majority of visitors was concealed behind a semi-circle of blue curtains that hung from ceiling to floor, creating behind them a magical dolphin space. Dolphins' images swam to music in a pool surrounded by pebbles and sand. A rotating blue disc with clear panels, illuminated by a spotlight, projected flickering blue patterns that bounced off the walls and curtains, producing a visual impression of the sun dancing on a blue sea. It was a place in which to stand and experience an enchanting imaginary journey into the dolphin dreamland.

Had I seen the exhibition in London, New York or Paris, I would have been delighted. To experience it in Japan was unexpected and especially poignant. It gave me a feeling of optimism for the future.

Dolphin Odyssey attracted many visitors, one of whom, Kozue Yamada, gave me a postcard of an underwater picture she had taken of a Humpback whale and its calf off Hawaii. On the back it was inscribed:

We can learn from dead whales but there is always a limit. There are no limits to what we can learn from living ones.

She then told me she often swam with a school of friendly dolphins off the coast of Japan. This was exciting news for me and further softened my views of Japan and its people.

I enjoyed standing quietly in a corner of the gallery watching the expressions on the faces of the Oriental people who came in to gaze at the exhibits. They ranged from small groups of active schoolchildren to venerable old men with yellow parchment skins and grey goatee beards – ancient, owl-like sages, wise and serene, at peace with themselves and the world as they stood in front of the various exhibits quietly assimilating the legends and pictures.

One of the people I met in the exhibition was the Russian harpist, Antonina Krutikova, who was visiting Tokyo with the Moscow Chamber Musical Theatre. She told me in broken English how she had swum with wild dolphins in the Black Sea and had dreamed of them since childhood. I gave her the dolphin ring I had put in my pocket on impulse just before leaving England. The thought of the dolphin, another talisman, dancing across the strings of her harp was an image that sat comfortably in my imagination.

Before we parted company I told Antonina (or Ata, as she preferred to be called) that I hoped the ring might inspire her to write some dolphin music. She had glorious golden hair and eyes of sparkling blue. But her brow furrowed and her expression was heavy when she talked about the serious situation in her own country, which was then in a state of political and economic turmoil. She spent a long time alone, tears sliding down her cheeks, in the curtained-off area of the exhibition. She was a changed person after her Tokyo experiences. So was I.

· 17 ·

Energy Channels

What is Ki, Chi, or Qi? My first inquiries suggested that
these were three words for the same almost indefinable thing
– the life force energy that is still, after centuries, the main-
stay of orthodox Chinese medical practice. It couldn't be
measured, I was told. No one could offer me in Western
terms an acceptable scientific definition. Perhaps, like God, it
was something personal to each individual. Or was I running
on the wrong track altogether? Was it, like the Dreamtime,
one of those eternal mysteries beyond the boundaries of language but not beyond the human mind?

These questions did not deter me; in fact they did the
opposite. I went back to basics. My own understanding of
how the body worked and responded to treatment was
rooted in textbooks I had studied before and after my PhD –
Gray's Anatomy, Samson Wright's Applied Physiology and
Pharmacology for Medical Students. There were no clues to
be found in these.

'It is no wonder,' Shizuko told me. 'Western medicine
begins with a corpse. Your medical students dissect dead
bodies, separate nerves and blood vessels. They base
treatment on this knowledge. Then they use chemicals.
These are all dead things. In Chinese medicine we start with
a living body. Ki energy is what keeps it alive. Without Ki it
dies. In China medical students start by studying Ki.'

Since my training there has been a new awakening in the
West to alternative approaches to healing based on natural
remedies. This change of attitude was fostered by the
popular press. On 18 June 1992 the *Daily Telegraph* reported

the inauguration of the British Complementary Medicine Association.

The *Sunday Times Magazine* made several references to Ki in a series of articles on traditional Chinese medicine. Many of the alternative methods now being employed in the West are derivations of practices that came from ancient Eastern cultures. Acupuncture appears to work but no one knows exactly why.

Someone I met at the *Dolphin Odyssey* exhibition set a corner of the jigsaw for me. Maya Moore was nearly six feet tall with distinctly Japanese features. When she asked me about one of my pictures which was hanging in the exhibition I didn't know that she was a television presenter for 'World News Europe', broadcast on NHK Satellite from Paris, nor that she was preparing to host a new TV series featuring famous conservationists such as Harrison Ford and Robert Redford. Maya told me she had spent four years in England and had studied Ki Gong in Taiwan under the guidance of a big Vietnamese monk whom she described as being like a massive tree with large limbs and strong spreading roots.

At the end of the course the monk told Maya that she could control Ki (or Chi, as he called it) and, to prove it, he handed her one end of a four-foot-long steel rod of the type used for reinforcing concrete. Holding the other end in his cupped hands, he instructed Maya to rest her end at the bottom of her throat, in the dip at the top of her breast-bone, and then walk towards him. She did so without hesitation. The metal rod bent like a hairpin. Maya was convinced that it was not she but the monk who somehow had caused the bar to bend as if it were made of plasticine. Why should she tell me such a story if it were not true? I could see no reason why I should disbelieve her, but I wanted to find out more.

A breakthrough came when I discovered a book published in the mid-Eighties, called *Encounters with Qi, Exploring Chinese Medicine*, which gave a fascinating insight into medical practices that went back to the Yellow Emperor, who was believed to have lived around 2700 BC. The author, Dr David Eisenberg from Harvard Medical School, was the first American medical exchange student to visit the People's Republic of China where, in 1979, he studied traditional Chinese medicine for a full year. His text confirmed what Shizuko had been telling me. Eisenberg admits 'I found it difficult to dissociate from my background and my Western biomedical bias.'

His teachers at the Beijing Institute of Traditional Chinese Medicine set human anatomy in a new light with their interpretation of relationships between organs that derived from China's earliest physicians – the ancient philosophers. According to them, the kidneys control sexual activity and the lungs are responsible for the hair and the skin. To tie these apparently arbitrary relationships together, it was necessary for the American doctor to put aside what he had already learned and introduce Qi – the vital energy.

When Eisenberg confessed that he did not understand Qi, his tutor, Dr Fang, told him: 'Qi means that which differentiates life from death, animate from inanimate. To live is to have Qi in every part of your body. To die is to be a body without Qi. For health to be maintained there must be a balance of Qi, neither too much nor too little.'

After studying theory for two months Eisenberg replaced his stethoscope with acupuncture needles, and later attended a four-hour operation on a 58-year-old professor who had a large brain tumour removed under acupuncture anaesthesia. The patient talked to Eisenberg and remained conscious throughout. When surgery was completed, Professor Lu shook hands with the anaesthetist and walked out of the operating room unassisted.

Eisenberg met one Qi Gong Master who swallowed two iron balls, each weighing two-and-a-half pounds, and then brought them up again, spitting them out at his feet. This was a warm-up for his next feat, which was to crack open against his forehead two fist-sized stones. Eisenberg then watched the man move a lantern from three feet away using external Qi. The demonstrator admitted that there were Qi Gong practitioners who used strength and a knowledge of stress points to crack rocks, but this was not true of the great

Qi Gong Masters who could perform feats that relied only minimally on physical strength.

Some Qi Gong Masters used external Qi instead of needles to stimulate important acupuncture points for pain-less surgery. When he himself was treated with external Qi, Eisenberg remarked that it was 'as if my hands had been plugged into a low voltage socket'.

Despite the fact that his Chinese hosts were clearly much more interested in the application of Qi than in identifying its physical nature, when pressed, they agreed to provide proof of its existence.

In a totally darkened room Eisenberg and a colleague, Herb Benson, saw a Qi Gong Master make a fluorescent tube glow brightly.

'What do you think, Herb?' Eisenberg asked. They agreed it could have been due to some form of static electricity.

'If you try to publish this sort of observation in any scientific journal critics would skin you alive,' added Benson.

I agree with that, and also with one of the final statements in Eisenberg's book which identified Qi Gong as 'the most perplexing of Chinese therapeutic interventions'. Eisenberg concludes:

> The art of healing is thousands of years old. The science of healing is still in the process of being born.
>
> Although the incidence of specific diseases in China differs from that in the West, the patients are by and large the same – suffering from the same symptoms, the same diseased organs, the same tormented psyches. The Chinese and Western medical models are like two frames of reference in which identical phenomena are studied. Neither frame of reference provides an unobstructed view of health and illness. Each is incomplete and in need of refinement.

One of the cornerstones of Chinese medicine is that environment, diet, behaviour, thought and emotions play an integral role in the maintenance of health. Millions in China today practice Qi Gong, or Tai Chi, exercises daily.

The Chinese idea that human psyche can influence susceptibility to disease and the course of an illness is now being taken seriously in the West. Do meditation, biofeedback, faith and the relaxation response alter human physiology? My personal view, based on what in science would be termed 'anecdotal evidence', is that they do. Research workers in behavioural science, psychosomatic medicine, endocrinology and neurology are banding together in multidisciplinary investigations to provide data that will satisfy the doubters. They have even created a new branch of science and called it psychoneuroimmunology!

How long will it be before the existence of Ki will find widespread acceptance, especially in medical schools? I suspect not long, for the concept that Eastern and Western forms of medicine are mutually exclusive is breaking down. Our minds are opening rapidly to new possibilities that earlier would have been dismissed as utterly ridiculous. For instance, which reputable publisher even a few years ago would have agreed to bring out a serious book entitled *Dolphins and their Power to Heal*? Yet a colourful, informative, well-researched volume on this topic by Amanda Cochrane and Karena Callen, both highly respected writers, appeared in the bookshops from a mainstream publisher in April 1992.

In their opening pages Cochrane and Callen succinctly report on the beneficial effects of dolphins on people which I first observed in the 1970s and later explored in Operation Sunflower:

> Dolphins seem to possess the power to make an impression on, or reawaken, our emotional centre, which resides in the limbic system, one of the most primitive regions of the brain. Feelings of both pleasure and pain can be triggered by stimulation of this area.
>
> Many people who have entered into a state of depression because they are unable to cope with life suffer from an emotional anaesthesia which effectively prevents them from feeling either pleasure or pain, as they have lost sight of the emotional side of their lives. A similar suppression

of emotion is also characteristic of many cancer patients. They have poorer outlets for emotional discharge. A clinical psychotherapist, Dr Lawrence LeShan, has been studying the relationship between personality and illness. His investigations have revealed an inextricable link between despair and the onset of cancer. LeShan believes that those who suppress their emotions, whether these be of anger, sorrow, pleasure or frustration, are more likely to develop certain forms of cancer. His research has been backed up by Dr A.H. Schmale and Dr H. Iker at the University of Rochester in New York State, USA. Studies also reveal that negative mental attitudes suppress the immune system, thereby leaving the body open to attack from disease.

While it may be possible to use drugs to numb pain or artificially reproduce feelings of pleasure, the effects of such substances are shortlived and can bring on much worse symptoms of withdrawal. Our experiences with dolphins suggest that by contrast, whether the animals bring on feelings of euphoria or tears, they are exerting an essentially natural, safe and positive therapeutic influence.

As well as providing some perceptive material on endorphines and other chemical changes that take place in people when they are submerged in water, and on the dolphin's complex sonar system and the healing power of sound, the book pinpoints the energy connection that I had been seeking:

It is our belief that dolphins exert their healing influence on people on a subtle energetic level, and researchers working at the forefront of dolphin healing are beginning to substantiate this notion. All creatures have energy fields that extend beyond their physical body. These force fields are explained in scientific terms by the fact that the brain and the associated nervous system are run by electrical signals. Whenever electrical energy flows, it generates an electrical field. It was Harold Saxton Burr, an American researcher and Professor of Anatomy at Yale University

Medical School, who discovered overall body fields in men and women as well as in animals, trees, plants and raw protoplasm when investigating the electrical phenomenon in the 1940s. He called these fields bio-electrical or electro-dynamic L fields – the fields of life . . .

Burr spent some time working with Yale University psychiatrist Dr Leonard Ravitz, and proved without a doubt that emotions affect our life fields. The strength and quality of the field appear to be influenced by the electrical activity of the brain, or, in other words, by mental states. This helps to explain the potent influence of the mind on the health of the physical body. Burr and his colleagues also found that emotional instability is marked by a high L field. This discovery is borne out by the fact that brain wave frequencies are also higher in manic states, which in turn lends credence to the Chinese idea that an energy imbalance showed that mind, body and soul were not in harmony and was an early warning sign that disease was imminent.

This brings me back to Professor Nakagawa. In order to understand how his healing techniques relate to dolphin therapy firstly we have to acknowledge that his methods work. He can produce hundreds of patients who will testify to this. Secondly we have to accept the existence of the life force Ki. Having done that, we must create a mental picture that will enable us to visualise what is happening. My own way of doing this is to think of the human body as incorporating a complex system of invisible conduits through which energy flows. These are not physically discernible in the way that blood vessels are. Yet over the centuries their courses have been charted and shown to link various organs, their routes being different from those followed by nerves. The conduits close to the surface are the well-documented meridians that are used in acupuncture.

I visualise this network as a drainage system. The pipes through which the water (representing Ki energy) passes remain clear if there is a regular movement back and forth.

But if stagnation or breakdown occurs, then a blockage, partial or total, is likely to form. When this happens the organ at the end of the line is deprived of the energy needed to keep it healthy and it malfunctions, or ceases to work altogether.

Some of the energy conduits are like drains under the road that can be accessed via drain covers which act as switches. These correspond to the pressure points in the meridians into which acupuncture needles are inserted. The needles act as connectors allowing energy (or water in the drainage system analogy) to flood into the system and clear the appropriate line.

In normal circumstances there are numerous methods of keeping the energy flowing. Those related to breath are especially important and contribute to the health-promoting and therapeutic value of chanting, singing and deep breathing exercises. When the body is unduly stressed, physically or emotionally, the energy pipes constrict and this limits the flow of Ki energy. During sleep, meditation and altered states of consciousness the pipes are able to dilate to their normal capacity, healing the body in the process.

When Ki Gong masters, or healers such as Nakagawa, treat their patients, they teach them first to relax, which dilates the channels. Patients then participate in gentle exercises, usually waving arms in the air, which pumps the Ki energy back and forth. When they go into altered states of consciousness their metaphorical drain covers are lifted (switched to open) and the necessary Ki energy can be taken in to restore balance, either directly from the atmosphere or from the healer who acts as an external channel.

How, you ask, does this apply to dolphins?

The dolphins, being conscious breathers, are constantly recharging themselves with Ki. Having the same brain size as humans, they are able to relate to us mentally in ways which other animals cannot. They can sense our emotions. People who feel a strong affinity with dolphins have their metaphorical drain covers open and are able to receive the Ki energy as soon as they come near a dolphin. Those listening to the audio-tapes move into a dolphin-like space and do likewise but take in the Ki energy either directly from the atmosphere or channelled by dolphins far away – like taking a long-distance telephone call.

My hunch is that dolphin Ki enters mainly through the crown chakra on the top of the head, but I have no proof of this. After the Ki energy balance has been restored the auto-immune systems function normally.

· 18 ·

Encounters with the Gods

When Wally and Trish Franklin invited me to sail with them
on a square-rigged ship to study Humpback whales in
Hervey Bay in August 1991 – part of their ten-year research
Oceania Project – I suddenly saw a unique opportunity for
Nakagawa and me to get together to investigate the source
of Ki. Having got Wally's consent to the Japanese healer
joining the expedition, I put the idea to Nakagawa in the
form of a proposal for a new film entitled *Hunt for Whale
Ki*. Typically, he had his own ideas and thought that any
attempt at measuring Ki, which had been elusive for 2,000
years, was not practical. Instead he wanted to do something
that was within his capabilities – communicate, no less –
with the whales and dolphins! He could not do this directly,
he told me, but it was possible through highly psychic third
parties. He would locate suitable mediums among the hundreds of likely candidates he encountered in the course of his
workshops. Furthermore, on finding the best candidates, he
would train them for this special task.

Arrangements were made for us to board *Svanen* at
Hervey Bay in Queensland on Saturday 31 August 1991, the
beginning of the eight-week season during which Humpback
whales were in the vicinity.

Svanen (The Swan) was a magnificent three-masted bar-
quentine, one of the world's few remaining timber sailing
ships. Built in Denmark in 1922 with Danish oak frames, she
started life as a grain carrier and continued in that role until
1969, when she was refitted and used as a training vessel by
the Royal Canadian Sea Cadets. After appearing at the

World Expo in Vancouver in 1986, *Svanen* sailed to England
to join the Australian Bicentennial First Fleet Re-enactment
for the historic voyage to Sydney, where she was now based.

Wally and Trish Franklin, who had dedicated themselves
to a greater understanding of the great whales, felt that the
best way to do this was to spend time with them in as unob-
trusive a manner as possible. What better way of doing so
than from a wooden square-rigged sailing ship, powered by
the wind, on which it would be possible to experience the
rhythms of the sea? Only a few people knew that they had
to put their house in Byron Bay on the market in order to
finance the Oceania Project. Wally told me it was an act
of trust on their part in the whales and dolphins.

The Oceania Project provided a number of free places on
the *Svanen* for researchers and deprived youngsters, and for
the operation to break even all the remaining spaces had to
be filled by paying guests. One such person who booked on
to the trip was Danni Olivier, who also reserved places for
her three children – Rebecca, age 11; David, age 19; and
Kirsty, age 21. In order to join the trip Danni gave up her
job, and by chance booked for the same week that I was to
be aboard. It was a decision that would profoundly change
the lives of her entire family.

An inkling of what was to come took place at the Harbour
View Caravan Park where we all stayed on the night before
embarkation. Danni and her family met the Japanese group
and joined in the Ki session that Nakagawa performed
outside his Camp-O-Tel as part of his programme to
raise the sensitivity of the two psychic students who were
to communicate with the whales and dolphins. The Olivier
family sat on the ground along with Nakagawa's team which
consisted of Shizuko, translator, Yasuhisa Oharada, a freelance journalist and photographer, and the two mediums
or channellers: Hiromi Kitzawa, a young single lady who
worked in a Japanese bank, and Shūko Semba, a piano
teacher and mother of two children. Also taking part were
Maya Moore who, after our meeting in Tokyo, had decided
to join the expedition with her sister Sara.

All those gathered, including the Australian family, were receptive to Nakagawa's power. Danni, with her eyes closed, sat cross-legged and swayed gently from side to side. Nakagawa – short, stocky, bespectacled, grey-haired, with a goatee beard – was held in high esteem by his young acolytes who were always in his company. In Japanese society, they would have accorded him respect for his age alone. Although he was less inscrutable than most of his generation, he nevertheless appeared somewhat remote to those who were not familiar with the Japanese.

In stark contrast to the professor was the captain of the *Svanen*, Jay D'Ambrumenil. You knew where you stood with him. He had risen rapidly to take command of the ship at the age of 22 through competence and force of character. He was a no-nonsense man, short-tempered, tough in body and character but with no malice, and not without a sense of humour. He ran a tight ship, as they say, and had brought the *Svanen* safely through some terrifying storms. The crew liked and respected him.

I doubt if Nakagawa fully realised what he was letting himself in for when he agreed to participate in the expedition. His edification began soon after we went on board the *Svanen*, which was moored in deep water outside the breakwater at Urangan in Hervey Bay.

We assembled on deck amidst a bewildering forest of ropes and were greeted by the captain who welcomed us aboard. He told everyone that they were invited to participate in the running of the ship, which included climbing aloft, setting the sails and swabbing the decks. In case anyone felt disinclined to volunteer, a duty roster had been prepared in which all guests on board, including Nakagawa, were delegated spells of cleaning the heads (the toilets), preparing food, washing up and keeping watch at night.

If Nakagawa felt inclined to delegate some of the more tiresome of these tasks to his subordinates, he could not avoid the communal living that is part and parcel of living on a basic sailing ship. His allocated bunk was in the middle of the saloon and could be reached only by clambering over a bench. It was situated directly opposite the head which was flushed by a noisy hand pump. Privacy consisted of a flimsy curtain which he could pull across while resting in his bunk. Everything else was open to view.

Professor Nakagawa was accustomed to the respect accorded to persons of such high standing in Japan. He stayed at luxury hotels when he travelled abroad. Now he was expected to spend the next five days locked in a floating box in the company of a motley assortment of strangers, most of whom were from Australia – not a country renowned for its social graces or the fine lines of protocol which were so important in Japanese society. Although he never revealed his feelings to me I realised the moment he boarded the *Svanen* that it must have been a testing culture shock for him.

The voyage of the *Svanen* was to be a learning experience not just for the Japanese but for everyone on board.

It began explosively on the first evening, and took everyone by surprise. Spontaneously, and without any warning, the unexpected took place.

Having led many expeditions in the past, I was familiar with the bewilderment experienced by such groups when they first come together. There was always the need for a settling-in period. So I adopted my usual practice of making sure that everyone got to know each other. When our first evening meal was over and the crew had retired to their quarters for the night, I assembled the other guests in the saloon and showed them a video of *The Dolphin's Touch*. We talked for a while about Operation Sunflower and then I asked each person in turn to say who they were, why they had come, and what they hoped to get out of the voyage.

Everything went smoothly until it came to Nakagawa's turn. He spoke quietly about Ki and Shizuko translated. He then started to demonstrate how he generated Ki energy, whereupon his two psychic students went immediately into a trance, rocking violently with their bodies and gesticulating with their arms. They said there was an evil spirit on board.

After meeting Danni and her family, Nakagawa had sensed that she was suffering. He asked the mediums if the spirit was associated with Danni. With their eyes tightly shut and continuing their vigorous movements, they confirmed that the spirit was with her. When Shizuko asked Danni if she had any problems, she said that six weeks earlier her son Andrew, the twin of David who was in the saloon with us, had been tragically killed in a motor-cycle accident. Shizuko, who had worked with Nakagawa many times and knew that he would want to help Danni, suggested that she lay on the table and allow him to give her some healing energy. This she did, and went into a semi-conscious state while Hiromi and Shūko continued to communicate with the spirits.

From the questions asked by Nakagawa through Shizuko, the utterly bemused onlookers learned that Andrew (or Andy, as he was known) had been dotty about dolphins and always wore a dolphin effigy round his neck. His sudden and violent death had been traumatic for the entire family. The two mediums were still hysterical, and Shizuko explained that they were being entered by the evil spirit which had caused the accident. At that moment the captain, who had been woken from his sleep by the noise, entered the saloon. The spectacle he saw in the half-light was like that of a voodoo ceremony, with two wailing women thrashing around in a trance under the spell of a Japanese witch-doctor who had an Australian woman laid out on a table as if she were on a sacrificial altar. It was not the kind of thing he expected aboard his ship. I could see he was angry and was about to demand that it should stop. I went over to him and with some difficulty led him away from the scene.

I scarcely understood precisely what was happening. Could Danni be in danger if the strange exorcism that appeared to be taking place was brought to an abrupt end? Summoning up all my persuasive power, I told the captain what I thought was going on and urged him to calm down and not to break up the meeting at this critical moment. Grudgingly he consented, but said if it didn't stop soon he would take the matter into his own hands. Before returning to the saloon I tried to reassure one of the research scientists who, awakened by the noise, had got out of her bunk and was clearly agitated by what was going on.

Back in the saloon Shizuko was explaining that an evil spirit which had been lurking in Danni's body was being drawn out by the two mediums. Suddenly Nakagawa produced a Polaroid camera and took a flash picture which, when it self-developed a few minutes later, consisted mainly of a cream-coloured cloud with two horns which he said was the evil spirit. When the spirit eventually departed about five minutes later, his photographer, Yasuhisa Oharada, took another flash photograph with the same camera which produced a perfectly normal picture of Nakagawa's back.

Throughout all this the only recognisable English word the Japanese psychics used several times was 'Muma'. This, Danni said afterwards, was the way in which her son Andy had always addressed her.

I was relieved when things quietened down and everyone dispersed to their bunks. It was hard to make sense of what had taken place. We were all in a state of shock. It would certainly take time for my scientifically trained mind to assimilate just what had happened to Danni and her children.

One of those on board with whom I quickly established a good rapport was a 20-year-old cameraman whom Estelle had brought along to make a video of the expedition, which she saw as an important part of what she called 'the bigger picture'. Taylor Fogelquist was born of American parents in London and was still at college in the United States. Despite his youth, Taylor was widely travelled. He was open, cheerful and willing to take part in whatever was asked of him. I was never consciously aware of the generation gap between us and during the days that followed we spent

15 When I joined the Oceania Project, I discovered the ultimate
way in which to watch dolphins – from the square rigged
sailing ship *Svanen*

16 (*Above*) Professor Nakagawa puts one of his highly psychic students into a trance so as to communicate with the whales and dolphins

17, 18 According to Nakagawa, this Polaroid picture was an evil spirit leaving Dani's body (*below left*). A few moments later the same instant camera produced an unfogged picture of Nakagawa

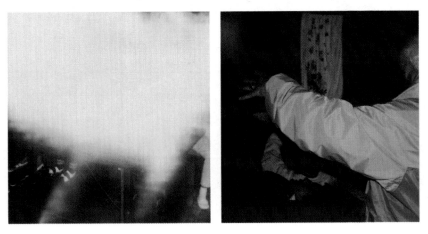

19, 20, 21 Huge Humpback whales breaching and cracking the surface with their scythe-shaped pectoral fins were an awesome sight

22 Dolphin bliss – JoJo and Dean

many periods together, discussing the film and the extra-ordinary events that were unfolding around us. Perhaps because his mind was more flexible than mine, Taylor was able to accept what was going on more readily than I was. One of the things he said stuck in my mind.

'Horace, what is happening here is a lesson to teach us that we must let go – of the past and the future.'

I could understand the idea of letting bygones be bygones, but the concept of letting go of the future was new to me. The past was solid, tangible, full of events. I had written about it in my books. I could throw a book away. The future didn't exist. Or did it? When I thought about it I realised that I knew many people whose everyday lives were governed by what might occur in the future. They took out insurance policies on life and possessions, were preoccupied with what might happen to their shares if the stock market collapsed, what if there was a war, how would they cope if they fell seriously ill. All those 'if's. According to my Snowman Principle, merely by having the thoughts, they were increasing the chances of those events actually taking place.

Taylor was right. We did have to let go of the future. And there was more to it than adopting the adage – *think positively*. Although that is exactly what I advised Shizuko to tell Nakagawa to do when she said on day two of the expedition that he was seriously questioning the value of his presence. The hostility and scepticism he had aroused unintentionally the night before had not gone unnoticed by the venerable healer, who said he had hundreds of patients anxiously waiting for treatment in Tokyo. Had we not sailed well away from the mainland and anchored off Fraser Island, I think Nakagawa might well have insisted on catching the next flight back to Japan. Shizuko reassured him. What was commonplace to him was totally new and to some extent frightening to the rest of those on board. She told him that he had my support, and that of Trish and Wally Franklin, who could see a connection between what he had done and the healing ceremonies performed by Australian Aborigines.

After that, with good grace, Nakagawa unobtrusively performed three or four Ki sessions a day which were always attended by his entourage, and in which anyone else could participate. The first of these took place on the deck after breakfast the next morning. I perched on a hatch cover and allowed myself to fall under his spell. Sitting cross-legged and with my eyes closed, I rocked gently from side to side. It was an eerie feeling. I was floating in the sky, which was pale blue, but at the same time I was conscious of what was happening around me on the ship, and that the two mediums were talking to the whales.

When later I took Shizuko to one side and asked her to explain what had happened, she said that Nakagawa acted like a gatherer of energy from the universe which he dispensed from his finger tips.

'In other words,' she said, 'he is an energy channel. He energises the mediums to the same level as the whales. Then the whale energy can flow into them and they become whale spirits. Their bodies become lighter and separate. Their consciousness remains a spectator but no longer has control over their physical state. Their bodies are occupied by the spirits of the whales and dolphins. You can ask them anything you like.'

Watching Hiromi and Shūko, I gained the distinct impression that they really were possessed by whale and dolphin spirits, and, unlike me, were totally unaware of where they were or what they were doing. They gabbled in Japanese while Shizuko plied them with questions from the group who stood around watching. From what the two channellers said, it seemed that the dolphins in particular had a sense of humour and sometimes gave funny answers, not always precisely to the question asked. As we were on a dolphin- and whale-watching trip, the questions most frequently asked were, 'Where were they?' and 'When would we see them?'

Shizuko was completely caught up in the theatre of the occasion. She became very dolphin-like herself. 'We are coming, we are coming,' she said urgently. 'But we are far away. Far away. We are coming. We are coming as quickly as we can. We don't know exactly when we will be with you. But wait. Please wait.'

The whales, however, said they would be with us soon. This the sceptics saw as no big deal, for we were in the right place at the right time to see Humpback whales on their northerly migration from Antarctica.

Meals were taken alfresco. After breakfast the decks were swabbed down, more to prevent the timbers from cracking in the sun than to wash away scraps of dropped food. When the chores were done, Wally Franklin usually climbed the stern mast and remained there for hours, acting as whale lookout. Those on the deck far below were occupied with their assigned tasks of the day or simply lolled in the shade reading a book.

It wasn't long before Wally shouted 'Whale-ho!' and pointed to a spot on the horizon. With the engine quietly throbbing below deck, we were soon under way and heading in the direction of his still-raised arm. Further cries from the masthead indicated that whales were popping up all over the bay. Either nature, or Nakagawa's magic, or both, were working well. In the distance we could see plumes of white foam, forming and disappearing like transient seagull's wings, as the giant Humpbacks heaved themselves high out of the sea in torrents of cascading water before falling back and sending clouds of spray skywards. It was a magnificent sight that we were to see time and again.

Captain Cook witnessed the same sights. 'With its whole body out of the water several times, making splash and foam as if a mountain had fallen into it,' was how his naturalist, Joseph Banks, recorded the behaviour in his diary over 200 years earlier. Commercial whale-watching, however, did not begin in Hervey Bay until 1987. It started after Brian Perry, who used to take visitors out on fishing trips, saw a trio of Humpbacks performing their activities in Platypus Bay. He put a small advertisement in the local paper declaring that he would take passengers to see whales on the first day of September. Such was the response that, three years later, the Queensland National Parks and Wildlife Services declared the area a Marine Park and limited and licensed the number of vessels allowed to take passengers on whale-watching cruises. They also established guidelines for conduct around the whales. One of the rules imposed was that vessels must not approach close to a whale.

The skipper of the *Svanen* observed this code of conduct. But some of the whales showed a distinct disregard for the protocol. On our third day out a solitary whale decided to investigate us. I watched in awe as it approached.

Although another Park rule held that nobody was to swim with the whales, Estelle had gone to considerable lengths to obtain special dispensation for me. I hesitated for a moment. I was unlikely to get another chance like this. Although the whale appeared to be moving slowly I knew that to be an illusion due to its size. It could be gone again in a few moments. I made up my mind to go in. Hastily I put on fins, mask and snorkel. The quickest way to get into the sea was to jump overboard, but that could frighten the whale. So gently I lowered myself over the side and entered the water with barely a splash. I looked to see which way the whale was travelling and decided on an interception course.

With firm strokes I swam away from the side of *Svanen* – and safety. Head down, I could see the sunlight reflected by the waves sweeping back and forth like searchlights in the cobalt blue depths. The whale was not visible through the water. I tilted my head back. Peering through the mask, my eyes just above the surface, I caught sight of a black silhouette, big as a submarine, with a tiny curved dorsal fin perched on a humped back. I put my head down and finned as hard as I could, hoping the whale would come into view below the surface. But it didn't. With underwater visibility at about ten metres, I raised my head again. The whale was scarcely more than fifty metres away, but the gap was closing fast.

A few moments later I was looking diagonally down at the head of the benign behemoth just beneath the surface. It was like suddenly finding myself in the presence of the biggest oak tree ever to exist in the forest.

It could have flicked me away like a fly with its enormous flukes. Instead it looked at me. Profoundly peaceful, the gaze from that small unblinking eye expressed nothing but gentle benevolence. I felt I was looking through a peephole into a vast dim cavern of wisdom and sadness. No treaty ever contrived by man could convey the offer of reconciliation in that whale's eye. I saw it only briefly, but I saw it. It planted an image in my mind and was gone. There followed the sight of a giant, scythe-shaped, barnacle-encrusted pectoral fin, edged with white. It stroked the water with the lazy motion of an albatross wing and passed by. The great body moved silently past, dark and seemingly endless. Then came the tail, as wide as a tennis court. One slow, sinusoidal undulation was all it took to propel the leviathan from sight. I watched the trailing scalloped edge of the tail fin vanish in the dark blue haze, leaving me alone in the ocean, surrounded by the harbingers of fear – the unseen and unknown.

I looked to the left, to the right and down towards the unfathomable depths into which the whale had disappeared. I had felt strangely safe and reassured in its presence. Now I was suspended over an empty blue void with only the air in my lungs separating me from oblivion.

I hung on the surface of the sea, another piece of flotsam slowly rocking in the heaving swell. Then I heard it – a sound welling up from the depths, a long mournful cry. In my excitement and rush to meet the whale I had blocked out all other sensations. Now, in my quiet loneliness, I could hear it. The song of the Humpback whale was all around me. I could feel it inside. It awakened a deep primeval sense. I was not just listening to the song – I was part of it. The whale was singing to me and I was the song.

I was lost in the Dreamtime. Those on *Svanen* watched.

The ship was not under sail and the engine was out of gear. It was a quarter of a mile off and still drifting away from me. I began the long, hard swim back.

The bosun came up to me when I climbed on board, my legs weak with exhaustion.

'The captain wants a word with you.'

I dried myself and made my way to the chartroom.

'In future, don't jump overboard without letting me know.'

The captain was right to rebuke me. I apologised. It was an obvious safety rule I should have thought about before impetuously abandoning ship.

One rule I did obey was to shout 'Going aloft' whenever I climbed the rigging, though a deep-seated aversion to behaving noisily in public prevented me from doing so with any more force than was necessary for the nearest person to me to know what I was about to do. I didn't have the courage to scramble like a monkey right to the top of the main mast at my first attempt. This was because there was a platform about two-thirds of the way up. To get above it involved hanging like a bat on the ropes to negotiate the overhang. The final leg to the flag consisted of converging rope steps called ratlines which became so narrow at the top that it was only with difficulty that I could squeeze my foot on to the rope rung.

I loved being aloft when the engine was off, the ship under sail, and I could hear the wind sighing in the canvas billowing out below me. When I made it right to the top for the first time I imagined how much my granddaughter Rebecca would have enjoyed being there with me. She was like a squirrel when it came to climbing trees. We had many real adventures together, although we would have had to embark upon this particular hypothetical escapade without the knowledge of her mother!

One evening we were surrounded by whales while at anchor off Fraser Island. With my didgeridoo in its case slung across my back, I climbed to the cross-trees to salute the parting day. The mast swayed gently. I played as the sun disappeared and the sea became a sheet of hammered copper, painted red. The sound of the surf on the beach whispered across the water. Rocking slowly from side to side, I peered down through the tangle of ropes. In the middle distance a Minke whale was moving steadily forward. Estelle and Taylor rowed out to intercept it.

From high on the mast the black silhouette of the dinghy, with its extended oars and vee-shaped wake, reminded me of a water-boatman insect. I moved my head so that it was composed nicely amid the lattice of taut ropes and fixed the image in my memory by taking an imaginary photograph. The picture quickly turned into a movie sequence when two dolphins gambolled into frame and played around the dinghy.

Out to sea the sky was deep orange. Over the island, which was turning purple in the invading dusk, it was deep blue and darkening rapidly. The stars, primrose yellow, and getting brighter by the moment, swayed back and forth – an illusion created by the movement of my perch. I didn't climb down until the heavens were black.

That night I awoke to a strange sound. It filled the hull. The whales were singing and their song hung around me like a faint lullaby. I pressed my ear to the wooden planking alongside my pillow. It was like putting my head inside a hall in which the whales were putting on a concert. They filled my memory cells with their voices. The Aborigines said that great spirits sang the world into existence. I was adrift in the Dreamtime, dancing with whales as they journeyed through the night bathed in billowing plumes of phosphorescence. My spirit joined them as the parade passed by the *Svanen*, which lay on the sea as peacefully as a sleeping swan.

Shizuko was both my link with Nakagawa and my mentor in matters spiritual. I was a slow student, and it was not until we had had several impromptu tutorials together that I felt I was beginning to understand what she claimed was happening. She sometimes spoke of the spirits, or 'guest vibrations' as she also called them, as if they were children who were mischievous at times, but could also be evil.

'On the first night,' she said, 'Nakagawa energised Danni and the two girls to the same level so that the bad spirit, or whatever was in her, could leave through them. Nakagawa says traffic accidents do not just happen. They are caused by bad spirits. The spirit responsible for Andrew's death had caused other nasty accidents. It was a dark spirit. Such spirits are low vibrations. They need a body. Nakagawa channels beautiful white light that raises the spirits to such a high level that they no longer need a body and can go to where they belong.'

A person can be occupied by many spirits, Shizuko told me, and one of the dead boy's personal spirits had also entered his mother. It was a good spirit, though bewildered at first because it did not know that Andrew had died. It did not like the cold mortuary, wanted a body and eventually found Danni. It liked being inside her so much that it didn't want to leave. Also it wanted to warn Danni of the evil spirit. When the evil spirit departed the benevolent spirit, which had been raised to a higher plane by Nakagawa, was happy to leave also.

I asked Danni and her children what they thought of the extraordinary and unexpected happenings that had taken place on the *Svanen*. They were a close and affectionate family, each of them deeply affected by the death of Andrew in different ways. His twin brother, David, was the most severely hurt, keeping his sorrow bottled up. He changed perceptibly during the voyage and by the end had, I think, come to terms with it. His elder sister, Kirsty, who had studied Japanese, was open-minded about what had happened and accepted it. Danni spoke for the whole family when she said they all felt healed.

'I feel as if I have said goodbye to Andy,' she said. 'Over the sea, in the presence of whales and dolphins, just as Andy would have wanted.'

When I questioned Shizuko about the uniqueness of Nakagawa's power to heal, she assured me that many people have it, and that Nakagawa taught them how to use it at his seminars.

'Such people,' she said, 'can use the energy to heal others. Everyone can do it, but some are much better than others.

The healing energy quite often manifests itself as swirls of pure white light in photographs.'

Shizuko and Nakagawa had dozens of pictures, taken by different photographers, showing people encircled with white light, or Ki, energy – including one of her with me on the stage at the conference in Tokyo. She insisted that Nakagawa had a great sense of fun and was not averse to telling a joke against himself. She told me one of his stories which involved a pregnant dog that had been poisoned. Its owner wanted the bad spirit that had been responsible for the deed to be exorcised. This Nakagawa was able to do through one of his mediums, as he had with Danni. The spirit of the foetus also wanted to receive white light and leave – which it did. But then the unborn puppy's spirit returned.

'Why have you come back?' asked Nakagawa through the medium.

'I forgot my tail.'

'But you don't need a tail where you are going.'

'Oh, yes I do,' said the puppy. 'Without it, how can I laugh?'

This anecdote appealed to Shizuko's sense of humour. Her eyes shone and she chuckled like a Japanese dolphin.

On the fifth day of our expedition, the final one for Nakagawa, the sea was as flat as a bowling green. To avoid taking *Svanen* back to port, we decided to transfer the Japanese party to one of the whale-watching boats that came out every day. As we moved away from our overnight anchorage off Fraser Island two Humpbacks cruised slowly up to us and breached in unison about ten metres from the bow. There was tremendous excitement on board as everyone rushed forward, cameras clicking, to record the encounter.

We had discovered earlier that some whales took no notice of the ship and continued on their majestic progression without deviation, apparently quite indifferent to our presence. Others were distinctly curious. If these majestic creatures were not so huge, and in some ways alien with their black bodies heavily encrusted with grey barnacles, you would say they were friendly. The two off the bow were obviously so. The whales waved their fins in the air and thwacked them on the surface with glorious relish. It was like the last night of the London Proms – the finale of a wonderful experience that was building to an uninhibited climax of jubilation.

Furthermore it did not end when the whales moved away for they were replaced by a posse of dolphins. They flew along just beneath the line of cheering onlookers standing on the netting strung beneath the long bowsprit.

I was among them. Focusing my attention on a single dolphin, I timed how often it surfaced – once in about every two minutes. It was flying through the water as fast as I could run at full speed. I was stationary and tried holding my breath in unison with the dolphin which was speeding forward under glittering starbursts of sunlight. My lungs were bursting to inhale long before the dolphin surfaced for the first time. How did they do it? Efficiency, speed, grace, beauty – the dolphins had it all. At that moment any monitor measuring human joy would have gone off the scale.

Wally asked Nakagawa what had been the last message from the whales and dolphins.

'Peace,' said Shizuko, translating, with tears filling her eyes. 'They dream of peace for mankind and love between humanity and cetacea.'

Shizuko said that Nakagawa felt truly 'blessèd' and was an ambassador who would take the love of the dolphins back with him to the Japanese nation.

She stayed aboard the *Svanen* while her compatriots were ferried, waving and smiling, towards the *Moby Dundee* which was standing by to take them to the mainland. We saw the laden tender go alongside the white hull and watched them climb safely aboard. Suddenly an enormous Humpback whale reared high out of the water immediately alongside *Moby Dundee*, dwarfing Nakagawa. He stood there, slightly crouched, with arms forward and fingers outstretched, just as he had done in the saloon on the first night of our voyage. This time he didn't need mediums to communicate; he was looking directly into the eye of a mighty whale. We all knew how much could be said without words.

The *Moby Dundee* moved off. There was a lot of confusion in the water around the stern. The sea was exploding with dolphins. There were dozens of them. Some were leaping vertically upwards. Others were making bridges. Trailing behind the *Moby Dundee* in its wake was a whole caravan of dolphins. I had never seen anything like it. Nor had any of the crew or whale-watchers. Shizuko was shaking with emotion, the tears flowing down her cheeks.

'The dolphins have come. The dolphins have come,' she cried. 'Just like they said they would.'

Her faith in our mission, which had never wavered, was overwhelmingly reaffirmed.

Later, Wally said he had never witnessed anything like it during his two full seasons of whale-watching. To him, the dolphins were the messengers and the great whales held the wisdom.

Most of his observations had been made from the masthead. Unlike me he had not swum with a whale or the dolphins – which I was lucky enough to do on several occasions.

'What was it like for you?' he inquired.

'For me, swimming with dolphins was like flying with angels,' I replied. 'But my meetings with the whales were like encounters with the gods.'

Acknowledgements

This book only made it to first base because of the deciphering and typing skills of Kerry Davis who transmogrified a mound of paper covered with handwritten hieroglyphics into an immaculate manuscript – for which I thank her immensely.

Not every line can be claimed as all my own work, for I have quoted extensively from other writings that have helped me in my quest to understand dolphins. In particular, I must offer my profound thanks to my friend Heathcote Williams for allowing me to quote a long extract from his poem *Falling for a Dolphin*. I also appreciate the kind permission of Amanda Cochrane and Karena Callan to quote a long passage from their book, *The Healing Power of Dolphins*. Briefer insights appear in my text from the works of Burnam Burnam, Bruce Chatwin, David Eisenberg, Paul Gilbert and Paul Spong, for which I am grateful, as indeed I am for general background provided by other books listed in the Bibliography. For quotations from their letters, I acknowledge, also with thanks, Jeremy Beckett, John Farrar, Paul Gilbert, Debbie Jamieson, Joseph Keszi, Paul Martin, Sue Rush, Paul Spies and Kozue Yamada. In addition, I must thank Lynne Truss, for the passage from her feature in the *Independent on Sunday*, and Hugo Davenport, for an extract from his article in the *Weekend Telegraph*. Photographs have been kindly provided by other friends: Christine Callaghan (3), George Guthrie (10), Masoto Nakagawa (17), Yashuisa Oharada (18), Ross Isaccs (19, 20), Ivo Charles (21) and Terry Howson (9). The rest I managed to snap myself.

In the making of a film the role of the editor is invariably acknowledged. It does not usually happen in the case of books, in which the role is no less important. It pleases me to offer my grateful thanks to Tony Colwell, my editor at Cape, for all his help and encouragement. I should also thank Shirley Whitelam for reading the proofs with her customary sharp perception.

Bibliography

Anthony Alpers, *Dolphins*, London: John Murray, 1960.

Deva and James Beck, *The Pleasure Connection. How Endorphins Affect our Health and Happiness*, California: Synthesis Press, 1987.

George H. Bell, Norman Davidson and Harold Scarborough, *Textbook of Physiology and Biochemistry*, Edinburgh: E & S Livingston, 1961.

David Bohm, *Wholeness and the Implicate Order*, London: Routledge and Kegan Paul, 1980.

Robin Brown, *The Lure of the Dolphin*, New York: Aron Books, 1979.

Burnam Burnam (see David Stewart).

Tony Buzan and Terence Dixon, *The Evolving Brain*, Newton Abbot (Devon): David and Charles, 1978.

Bruce Chatwin, *The Songlines*, London: Jonathan Cape, 1988.

Amanda Cochrane and Karena Callan, *Dolphins and their Power to Heal*, London: Bloomsbury Publishing, 1992.

Jacques-Yves Cousteau, *Dolphins*, London: Cassell, 1974.

James Cowan, *Mysteries of the Dreaming, The Spiritual Life of the Australian Aborigines*, Bridport (Dorset): Prism Press, 1989.

Windsor Cutting, *Handbook of Pharmacology. The Actions and Uses of Drugs*, New York: Meredith Corporation, 1969.

Barbara Dewey, *The Creating Cosmos*, Inverness: Bartholomew Books, 1985.

Wade Doak, *Dolphin Dolphin*, Auckland: Hodder and Stoughton, 1981.

Wade Doak, *Ocean Planet*, Auckland: Hodder and Stoughton, 1984.

Wade Doak, *Encounters with Whales and Dolphins*, Hodder and Stoughton, 1988.

Horace Dobbs, *Follow a Wild Dolphin*, London: Souvenir Press, 1990 edn.

Horace Dobbs, *Save the Dolphins*, London: Souvenir Press, 1992.

Horace Dobbs, *The Magic of Dolphins*, Cambridge: Lutterworth, 1990.

Horace Dobbs, *Tale of Two Dolphins*, London: Jonathan Cape, 1987.

Horace Dobbs, *Dance to a Dolphin's Song*, London: Jonathan Cape, 1990.

David Eisenberg with Thomas Lee Wright, *Encounters with Qi: Exploring Chinese Medicine*, London: Jonathan Cape, 1986.

Bibliography

Adolphus P. Elkin, *Aboriginal Men of High Degree*, St Lucia: University of Queensland Press, 1945 and 1977.

Peter Evans, *The Natural History of Whales and Dolphins*, London: Christopher Helm, 1987.

Kalykulya Everard and Barbara Everard, *Australian Aboriginal Culture*, Canberra: Australian National Commission for UNESCO, 1974.

Frank and Betty Few, *The Stone-Axe Maker*, Adelaide: Rigby, 1966.

Karl-Eric Fichtelius and Sverre Sjölander, *Man's Place: Intelligence in Whales, Dolphins, and Humans*, London: Gollancz, 1973.

Ronnie Fitzgibbon, *The Dingle Dolphin*, Athlone: Temple Printing, 1988.

Elizabeth Gawain, *The Dolphin's Gift*, Mill Valley (California U.S.A.): Whatever Publishing, 1981.

Paul Gilbert, *Human Nature and Suffering*, Hove (Sussex): Erlbaüm Lawrence, 1989.

J.D.P. Graham, *Pharmacology for Medical Students*, Second Edition, London: Oxford University Press, 1971.

Arthur Guirdham, *The Psychic Dimension of Mental Health*, Wellingborough: Turnstone Press, 1982.

Jim Howes and Neil McLeod, *Little Bit Long Way*, Melbourne: National Museum of Victoria, 1986.

Eric Hoyt, *Orca, The Whale Called Killer*, Camden East (Ontario): Camden House Publishing, 1984.

Jennifer Isaacs, *Australian Aboriginal Music*, Sydney: Aboriginal Arts Agency, 1979.

Jennifer Isaacs, *Australian Dreaming. 40,000 Years of Aboriginal History*, Sydney: Lansdowne Press, 1980.

Cyril A. Keele and Eric Neal, *Samson Wright's Applied Physiology*. Twelfth Edition, London: Oxford University Press, 1971.

Jonathan King, *Australia's First Fleet. The Voyage and the Re-enactment 1788/1988*, Sydney: Robertsbridge, 1988.

M. Klinowska and S. Brown, *A Review of Dolphinaria*, Cambridge: Department of The Environment, 1986.

John Lilly, *Man and Dolphin*, New York: Doubleday, 1961.

John Lilly, *The Mind of the Dolphin*, New York: Doubleday, 1967.

Pat Lowe with Jimmy Pike, *Jilji. Life in the Great Sandy Desert*, Broome (Western Australia): Magabala Books, 1990.

Sean Mannion, *Ireland's Friendly Dolphin*, Dingle (Co. Kerry, Eire): Brandon Book Publishers, 1991.

Janet Mathews, *The Two Worlds of Jimmy Barker. The Life of an Australian Aboriginal 1900–1972*, Canberra: Australian Institute of Aboriginal Studies, 1980.

Joan McIntyre, *Mind in the Waters*, New York: Scribner, 1974.

Virginia McKenna, Will Travers and Jonathan Wray, *Beyond the Bars. The Zoo Dilemma*, Wellingborough: Thorsons, 1987.

Bibliography

Elaine Morgan, *The Scars of Evolution. What our Bodies Tell us about Evolution*, London: Penguin, 1990.

Paul G. Morrison & Tony Rylance, *Amble. The Friendliest Port*, Gateshead: Howe Brothers, 1988.

Estelle Myers, *Cross Your Bridges when you come to them*, Stanwell Tops (NSW, Australia): Estelle Myers, 1981.

Jolanda Nayutah and Gail Finlay, *Our Land Our Spirit. Aboriginal Sites of North Coast New South Wales*, Lismore: North Coast Institute for Aboriginal Community Education, 1988.

Jim Nollman, *Dolphin Dreamtime – Talking to the Animals*, London: Anthony Blond, 1985.

Richard O'Barry, *Behind the Dolphin Smile*, North Carolina (U.S.A.): Algonquin Books, 1988.

Joan Ocean, *Dolphin Connection. Interdimensional Ways of Living*, Kailua (Hawaii): Dolphin Connection, 1989.

Michael Odent, *Water and Sexuality*, London: Arkana (Penguin), 1990.

Michael Poynder, *Pi in the Sky – A Revelation of the Ancient Wisdom Tradition*, London: Rider, 1992.

A.W. Reed, *Aboriginal Legends. Animal Tales*, Frenchs Forest (NSW, Australia): Reed Books, 1987.

Ainslie Roberts and Melva Jean Roberts, *Dreamtime Heritage. Australian Aboriginal Myths*, Blackwood: Art Australia, 1989.

Frank Robson, *Pictures in the Dolphin Mind*, New York: Sheridan House, 1988.

Hugh Rule and Stuart Goodman, *Gulpilil's Stories of the Dreamtime*, Sydney: William Collins, 1987.

Peter Russell, *The White Hole in Time. Our Future Evolution and the Meaning of Now*, London: Aquarian Press, 1992.

Bernie Siegel, *Love, Medicine and Miracles*, London: Arrow Books, 1989.

Robert Stenuit, *The Dolphin: Cousin to Man*, London: J.M. Dent, 1969.

David Stewart, *Burnam Burnam's Aboriginal Australia, A Traveller's Guide*, Cottage Point: Angus & Robertson Publishers/Dolphin Publications, 1988.

Theodor Georg Heinrich (alias Karl) Strehlow, *Songs of Central Australia*, Sydney: Angus & Robertson, 1971.

George Trevelyan, *Summons to a High Crusade*, Forres (Grampian): The Findhorn Press, 1986.

Mark Tucker, *Whales and Whale Watching in Australia*, Canberra: Australian National Parks and Wildlife Service, 1989.

Heathcote Williams, *Whale Nation*, London: Jonathan Cape, 1988.

Heathcote Williams, *Falling for a Dolphin* (Illustrated edition), London: Jonathan Cape, 1990.

Timothy Wyllie, *The Deta Factor: Dolphins, Extra-terrestrials, and Angels*, New York: Coleman Publishing, 1984.

INFORMATION

International Dolphin Watch is a non-profit-making organisation with a worldwide membership which is kept informed about many dolphin-related topics through its journal *Dolphin*. Its members are part of a network through which information is passed about where direct contact with dolphins can be made. A wide range of items, including *The Dolphin Dreamtime* audio cassette and *The Dolphin's Touch* video, are available by mail order. The address is: International Dolphin Watch, Parklands, North Ferriby, Humberside HU14 3ET. Tel: (0482) 634914. Fax: (0482) 634914.

The British Complementary Medicine Association, St Charles Hospital, Exmoor Street, London W10 6DZ. Tel (081 964 1205).

Council for Complementary and Alternative Medicine, 179 Gloucester Place, London NW1 6DX. Tel: (071) 724 9103.

Institute for Complementary Medicine, PO Box 94, London SE16 1QZ. Tel: (071) 237 5165.

The Holistic Network publishes a directory containing articles and a comprehensive list of holistic practitioners and centres in Britain and Eire. Address: PO Box 1447, London N6 5JN. Tel: (081) 341 6789. Fax: (081) 348 4579.

Register of Traditional Chinese Medicine, 19 Trinity Road, London N2 8JJ.

International Register of Oriental Medicine, Green Hedges House, Green Hedges Avenue, East Grinstead, Sussex RH19 1DZ. Tel: (0342) 313106/7.

Cadeuceus is a journal devoted to alternative methods of healing. Editor: Sarida Brown, 38 Russell Terrace, Leamington Spa, Warwickshire CV31 1HE. Tel: (0926) 422388.

Global Link-Up, subtitled a network of expanding consciousness, publishes a wide variety of articles on bringing us into harmony with the planet and one another. Editor: Shauna Crockett Burrows, 51 Northwick Business Centre, Blockley, Gloucestershire GL5 9RF. Tel: (0386) 852167.

The journal *Here's Health* adopts an holistic approach to maintenance of health and treatment of illness. Editor: Bridget Le Good, EMAP Elan Ltd, Victory House, Leicester Place, London WC2H 7BP. Tel: (071) 437 9011. Fax: (071) 434 0656.